LIVING *by* FAITH

J. Vernon McGee

LIVING *by* FAITH

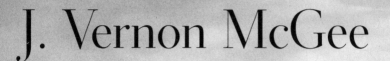

PRACTICAL LESSONS

FROM THE EPISTLE OF

JAMES

THOMAS NELSON PUBLISHERS®
Nashville

A Division of Thomas Nelson, Inc.
www.thomasnelson.com

Published in Nashville, Tennessee, by Thomas Nelson, Inc.

Library of Congress Cataloging-in-Publication Data

McGee, J. Vernon (John Vernon), 1904-1988
    Living by faith : practical lessons from the Epistle of James /
J. Vernon McGee.
      p. cm.
    ISBN 0-7852-6077-3
    1. Bible. N.T. James—Criticism, interpretation, etc. 2. Christian
life—Biblical teaching. 3. Faith—Biblical teaching. I. Title.
BS2785.6.C48M34 2004
227'.9106—dc22   2003024333

Printed in the United States of America
1 2 3 4 5 6 7 8 — 09 08 07 06 05 04

CONTENTS

INTRODUCTION

The Bible records several men by the name of James. So we ought to identify and introduce the James that we have in mind, and that is the one who wrote the Epistle of James. This James was our Lord's flesh-and-blood brother. He was a son of Mary and Joseph, which made him a half brother of the Lord Jesus. We find a reference to him in the Gospel of Mark:

> *Is this not the carpenter, the Son of Mary, and brother of James, Joses, Judas, and Simon? And are not His sisters here with us?* (Mark 6:3 NKJV)

I believe it was this same James whom Paul referred to in his epistle to the Galatians:

> *And when James, Cephas, and John, who seemed to be pillars, perceived the grace that had been given to me,*

they gave me and Barnabas the right hand of fellowship, that we should go to the Gentiles and they to the circumcised. (Galatians 2:9 NKJV)

This James is the man who we believe is the author of the Epistle of James.

His epistle opens with this:

James, a bondservant of God and of the Lord Jesus Christ . . . (James 1:1 NKJV)

I do not know about you, but I am confident that if I had been the Lord's half brother on the human side, somewhere in this epistle I would let the reader know it. I would have brought in that fact in a very casual and humble way, but I surely would have mentioned it. However, James did not do that. Instead, he called himself a bond slave of God and of the Lord Jesus Christ.

Our Lord Jesus was so human here on this earth that even His own brethren did not believe at first. They had been brought up with Him and seen Him grow up. They may have noticed that He was unusual, but they did not believe He was the Savior of the world. Of course, your family members are always the hardest people to reach; yet they are the ones we should reach.

James came to know the Lord Jesus not only as his blood

brother but as his own Savior, and then he became His bond slave. Notice what James called Him—he used His full name, the Lord Jesus Christ. James said, "He is my Lord." Jesus was His human name, and James knew Him as Jesus, his half brother; but he also knew Him as Christ, the Messiah who had come and died for the sins of the world.

In studying this epistle, we discover that James had a little different outlook on life from the one we have. The fact of the matter is that he seems to have nothing in common with the contemporary Christianity that we know today. I do not believe he would have very much to do with this frivolous and sophisticated type of fundamentalism that we have about us these days. He was austere, rugged, serious, and solemn. He was also very practical. He believed that Christianity had to be put in shoe leather, and if you couldn't put it in shoe leather, then it wasn't true Christianity. So he was very pragmatic.

The subject of his epistle is the ethics of Christianity, not doctrine or works, as many seem to think. He was discussing faith—a faith that works, my beloved. So he gave to us the skills and techniques necessary for living the Christian life faithfully.

ONE

THE ENTRANCE EXAMS
TO GOD'S UNIVERSITY

THE BOOK OF JAMES HAS BEEN compared to the Book of Proverbs in the Old Testament; both emphasize the practical aspect of living the Christian life, focusing on the learning experience for the child of God.

The Book of Proverbs is not just a series of sayings strung together like beads on a string. Rather, a story is told. There is, first of all, the appeal to the young man as he begins life by enrolling in God's school of wisdom. The young man matriculates in the school, the bell rings, the classes begin, and we see the development of the course throughout the Book of Proverbs.

The Epistle of James follows very much the same pattern. James enrolls the believer in the University of God. There are entrance exams to be taken, and they are not easy. The fact of the matter is, they are very difficult. It's a hard hurdle to clear. The lessons, first of all, are contrary to the thinking of the natural man. For that reason, the unsaved man could never qualify for these exams. This book was written to believers, so you must be a child of God to take these tests.

Let's imagine now that the bell has rung for the opening chapel, and "Dean James" is ready to give his first lecture, so let's listen in:

James, A servant of God and of the Lord Jesus Christ, to the twelve tribes scattered abroad [among the Gentiles in the dispersion]: Greetings (rejoice)! (James 1:1 AMPLIFIED)

"Rejoice" is the warm word of welcome James gives to believers as they enter the University of God. By the way, this university has another name: it's sometimes called the school of hard knocks. But James said, "Rejoice." In many ways, that is the key—the overtone and the undertone—of the Epistle of James.

All believers are candidates for a degree in God's University. In what field will we earn our degree? Well, there's only one field covered in this university. The subject is made very clear, yet many manage to miss it. I once heard a liberal lecturer speak on the Epistle of James, and he said that the theme was good works—and that James actually wrote his epistle to contradict and correct Paul the apostle, who emphasized justification by faith apart from works.

Well, James could not have written to correct Paul, for the very simple reason that James' epistle was the first book written in the New Testament. If there were any correcting to be done, Paul would have done it.

The theme of the Epistle of James is not works at all. The theme is faith. It's the same theme that Paul had, but James looked at it from a different viewpoint; he said that *faith produces works*.

When James discussed works, he was not talking about the works of the law, but of faith. We may put it like this: Paul talked about the root, which is faith; James discussed the fruit and works of faith. Therefore, our major in the University of God is faith; we are saved by faith, we grow by faith, we live by faith, and we die by faith. The child of God enters a life of faith the moment he trusts Christ, and that is the great theme that God teaches in His university.

We are saved by faith, we grow by faith, we live by faith, and we die by faith.

As the dean of God's University, James' first lecture is on the subject of faith—namely, the testing of faith through trials:

Consider it wholly joyful, my brethren, whenever you are enveloped in or encounter trials of any sort or fall into various temptations. Be assured and understand that the trial and proving of your faith bring out endurance and steadfastness and patience. (James 1:2–3 AMPLIFIED)

Is the Christian to experience joy through all the trials, troubles, and tensions of this life? The answer that I would give is *no*—that's not what James said here. Saying that you are reconciled to the will of God during times of trouble when you really are not reconciled leads to unreality in the Christian life. Many say that they are bowing before God's will and are accepting their trials with joy, but in their hearts is rebellion. They are not really reconciled to God. Instead, they are putting up a front and doing whatever it is they think a Christian *should* do. May I say to you, there are a lot of Christians today who seem to operate that way. But we are never asked to say that which is not really from the

> My *friend*, *you are not reconciled to the will of God until you can rejoice*—not *for the trials, but* in *them.*

heart. My friend, you are not reconciled to the will of God until you can rejoice—not *for* the trials, but because of them.

If I may be technical a moment, the Greek aorist tense used here suggests that the joy is *the result* of the trial. The idea that there is something joyful *in* the trials and tragedies of life is not true; trials come to us in order to bring joy into our hearts and lives. The writer to the Hebrews makes the mind of God very clear:

> **Now no chastening seems to be joyful for the present, but painful . . .** (Hebrews 12:11 NKJV)

Isn't that the truth? No chastening—and the word here actually refers to "child training," the discipline of a child—seems joyous when you are going through it. It's a form of insanity to say that you are finding pleasure in your troubles. Now, I do know some folk who seem to enjoy bad health—at least, they really enjoy telling you all about it! But that's an abnormal viewpoint.

James made it clear that trouble is not given to us for trouble's sake; it is never an end in and of itself. God always has a reason for testing us. The writer to the Hebrews continued:

> **Nevertheless, afterward it yields the peaceable fruit of righteousness to those who have been trained by it.**
> (Hebrews 12:11 NKJV)

"*Afterward* it yields the peaceable fruit of righteousness." Therefore, trials are meaningless, suffering is senseless, and testing is irrational unless there is a sound reason for and some good purpose served by them. When the external pressures of testing are upon us, and we are placed in the fires of adversity, calamity, tragedy, suffering, disappointment, or heartbreak, the internal attitude of faith should be that God has permitted it for a purpose, and He has a high and lofty goal in view. For "we know that all things work together for good to those who love God" (Romans 8:28 NKJV).

I must hasten to add that this doesn't mean that we will *understand* what purpose God has in it. The fact of the matter is, I'm of the opinion that we will not understand. This is the test of *faith*, "for we walk by faith, not by sight" (2 Corinthians 5:7 NKJV).

What are some of the purposes served in the testing of faith? Has God put down certain guidelines that give us an idea of why He permits trouble to come? Why He tests His saints today? Why He puts them into the fires of suffering?

TESTING PROVES THE GENUINENESS OF OUR FAITH

The testing of faith is proof positive of its genuineness. When your faith is tested, then you'll find out whether it's genuine or not. Notice that James began verse 3 of chapter 1 with "knowing that the testing of your faith . . ." (NKJV). God tests our faith that we might *know* it is genuine.

Let me illustrate. Some years ago, I had the privilege of leading to the Lord a secretary to one of the officers in a large airplane plant. On a number of occasions, she asked me to speak to a Bible study class in that plant. While I was there, I learned something of how air- planes are built. They start out by designing a new plane on the drawing board. Then blue- prints are drawn up, models are made, the models are tested, and then construction begins. After about two years, the first plane rolls off the assembly line. The question remains: Will it fly? Will it perform? Will it stand the test? So a test pilot puts the plane through the paces up in the air. Once the plane has proven to be all that the maker has said it is, there is con- fidence in the aircraft, and the airlines buy it. It is then brought to the airport where passengers board it, and the plane thus becomes serviceable and useful.

> *God tests our faith that we might* know *it is genuine.*

In the same sense, someone brings ore to an assayer to prove that it is gold or it is silver. The assayer puts a fire under it, pours acid on it, and then declares whether or not it is genuine.

Likewise, God puts faith to the test to prove that it is genuine. Someone has expressed it like this: "The acid of grief tests the coin of belief." There is a lot of truth in that.

When our Lord began His ministry, He encountered a group of folks who expressed a faith that proved to be false:

> *Now when He was in Jerusalem at the Passover, during the feast, many believed in His name when they saw the signs* [miracles] *which He did. But Jesus did not commit Himself to them, because He knew all men, and had no need that anyone should testify of man, for He knew what was in man.* (John 2:23–25 NKJV)

Did He suspect them? He surely did. He knew their belief was not genuine because He "knew all men." When a time of testing came for them, by the way, it was proven that theirs was not a genuine faith. Our Lord said to them later:

> *"But there are some of you who do not believe." For Jesus knew from the beginning who they were who did not believe, and who would betray Him. And He said, "Therefore I have said to you that no one can come to Me unless it has been granted to him by My Father." From that time many of His disciples went back and walked with Him no more.* (John 6:64–66 NKJV)

They couldn't stand the test, so they went away and left Him. Then our Lord turned to His own disciples, the Twelve, and asked them, "Do you also want to go away?" Simon Peter, answering for them, replied, "Lord, to whom shall we go? You have the words of eternal life" (John 6:67–68 NKJV). *Their* faith, you see, was genuine.

David was another whose faith was tested. That little shepherd boy went through a great deal of testing. In fact, I know of no other man who was ever tested quite like David. I imagine that when he was an old man sitting in the palace, he thought back over his life and remembered when he was a little shepherd boy out yonder on the hills of Bethlehem. When he looked at his life, he saw how God had led him, and that's when he wrote Psalm 23. Only a man who had been tested could write, "The LORD is my shepherd; I shall not want" (Psalm 23:1 NKJV). An inexperienced man who knew nothing about life could not have written that statement. But David, a man who had his life and his faith tested in the fires of adversity, could.

Paul the apostle was another man who was really tested. The fact of the matter is, he was told when he was called that he was going to be tested:

> **But the Lord said to him, "Go, for he is a chosen vessel of Mine to bear My name before Gentiles, kings, and the children of Israel. For I will show him how**

many things he must suffer for My name's sake." (Acts
9:15–16 NKJV)

Why did God test him so? It was so that no one since then
could say, "I'm enduring more than anyone else. Why does
God let this happen to me?" We may be suffering, or we may
think we are, but none of us suffer as Paul the apostle suffered
for the Lord. His faith was tested, and when he wrote the
Epistle to the Galatians he said:

> *From now on let no one trouble me, for I bear in my*
> *body the marks of the Lord Jesus.* (Galatians 6:17 NKJV)

He was no young theological professor raising questions
about the inspiration of Scripture and the reality of the
Christian faith. He was a man who *knew*.

My friend, if your faith is genuine, God will test you to
prove it. The church today is filled with shallow and super-
ficial saints. Why? They've never been tested. I recall reading a book by a brilliant theological professor. He was a
clever fellow, and he did some of the neatest tricks on a
mental trapeze that I've ever seen. But you couldn't read his
book without sensing that he had a feeling of insecurity.
Why? I suspect it's because his faith had never been tested.
In his writing, he put his faith through all kinds of intellectual gymnastics and made it perform like a trained ele-

phant. The only trouble with that is that faith is not a trained elephant, nor is it lived out on a mental trapeze. It must walk the streets of life in order to be real, my beloved. Faith must be tested; if it's not, then it is impossible to know for sure whether or not it is genuine.

We hear a lot from so-called intellectuals who question the Word of God. They raise all kinds of questions. Why? Their faith has never been tested. When your faith has been tested, you don't

> *Faith needs to be brought out of the ideal atmosphere and taken down to the streets where we live and move and have our being.*

argue about it, my beloved. Once a man has taken his ore to the assayer, it's been taken through the fire, the acid has been poured on it, and it's been beaten, do you think he'd waste even five minutes arguing with anybody about whether or not his ore is genuine? He *knows* it's genuine, because the test has been made.

My beloved, faith needs to be brought out of the ideal atmosphere and taken down to the streets where we live and move and have our being. God wants our faith to be tested in our lives. That is one of the reasons why He gives us an entrance exam of suffering or tragedy.

TESTING PRODUCES PATIENCE

There is a second reason and purpose in the testing of faith: it produces patience in the life.

> *Be assured and understand that the trial and proving of your faith bring out endurance and steadfastness and patience. But let endurance and steadfastness and patience have full play and do a thorough work, so that you may be [people] perfectly and fully developed [with no defects], lacking in nothing.* (James 1:3–4 AMPLIFIED)

You will never become patient by trying to be so out of your own will; nor will the Holy Spirit place it on a silver platter and offer it to you as a gift. Patience comes through suffering and testing.

Have you ever noticed the patience of dear saints who have been on beds of pain and sickness for years? They are long-suffering. And then others, who have not had to go through that, are so impatient. I recall a time when I was scheduled for an X-ray at the medical clinic. I sat waiting for a little under an hour, and then I went over to the receptionist and asked, "What's the matter?" She said to me, "Just be patient." Oh, my beloved, suffering and testing produce patience.

Notice that verse 4 says the testing is so that we might be "perfectly and fully developed." You will never be a perfect—that is, a complete and fully mature—Christian without patience. Some Christians have never really grown up but have remained babes. I made the statement as a pastor one Sunday morning that there were more babes in the church service than there were in the nursery downstairs. I tell you, I didn't get too many laughs from that comment. The difference, however, is that the babies in the nursery were beautiful, but the ones sitting in the church service were not very pretty! There is much clamoring and criticizing, turmoil and tension in our churches today. The reason is that many Christians have not grown up; they are still babes. God tests us so that we might grow up. David wrote something quite interesting:

Surely I have calmed and quieted my soul, like a weaned child with his mother; like a weaned child is my soul within me. (Psalm 131:2 NKJV)

That's what trouble and testing did for David! Have you ever noticed a baby when it's being weaned—how fretful it is, wanting to get back to the bottle? Then the day finally comes when the baby is weaned and is satisfied with solid food.

There are a lot of spiritual babes today who still want the bottle. When God takes the bottle away from them and begins to give them the good solid food of testing, they become very fretful. What's God doing? He's attempting to bring us to the place where David was when he was able to say, "I have quieted my spirit like a weaned child. I don't fret and cry all the time for the bottle." God tested David, and that testing enabled him to grow up.

What about you? Are you still on the bottle? Is God today trying to wean you? And are you fretting over the problems and difficulties and tensions of life? God is trying to produce patience in you. Paul confirmed this when he wrote to the Romans:

> *And not only that, but we also glory in tribulations, knowing that tribulation produces perseverance* [patience]; *and perseverance, character; and character, hope. Now hope does not disappoint, because the love of God has been poured out in our hearts by the Holy Spirit who was given to us.* (Romans 5:3–5 NKJV)

Now that's what you call a domino reaction! A great many people ask for patience, and when God sends them trouble, they say, "Lord, I didn't ask for trouble. I asked for patience." But that's precisely what He's doing; He's making you patient by sending you trouble. The domino reaction goes like this:

God sends us trouble so that we learn patience. Then patience eventually produces hope, and hope produces love (this is not our love for God but God's love for us), and that love is shed abroad in our hearts by the Holy Spirit.

Over the years of my ministry, I have seen the Holy Spirit work this out in the lives of many folk. I recall one man, who, when I first met him, was a real baby. He was loud, noisy, and critical. Oh, how difficult he was! Then trouble came, and I mean *trouble*. He passed through deep waters. He seemed crushed for a time, but I watched him slowly make a comeback.

He was different afterward; he was then one of the strongest and most stable believers I'd known. What happened? God tested his faith, and it was genuine.

TESTING PRESENTS A PROGRAM FOR THE FUTURE

There's another purpose in God's sending trials to us: it presents a program for the future.

> *Blessed (happy, to be envied) is the man who is patient under trial and stands up under temptation, for when he has stood the test and been approved, he will receive [the victor's] crown of life which God has promised to those who love Him.* (James 1:12 AMPLIFIED)

Testing is one of God's methods of developing us in the Christian faith. It is how He enables us to grow and develop patience in our lives down here, but He also has something in mind for the future: the "crown of life."

Testing of any kind, but especially if it is a severe calamity or tragedy, has a tendency to produce a miasma of pessimism and hopelessness. I do not blame a man whose wife is ill with Parkinson's disease for asking, "Why?" But the child of God can have the confidence that God is doing it for a very definite reason, and He has a purpose in it all.

> *When faith is tested and surrounded by darkness, when the waves are rolling high and all seems lost, the child of God knows that this is not the end.*

However, the man of the world will sink beneath the waves of adversity. Life, even at its best, makes him pessimistic. How many cynics are there today? How many are filled with bitterness, although they have everything? We are seeing an epidemic of suicides among teenagers, and thousands of other young people are dropping out of society today. Why? It is because they have no goal in life. A sensible news commentator once made the observation that back during the Depression, people had a will to live, and there were very few suicides. But today, when everything has been given to them, people want to die.

When faith is tested and surrounded by darkness, when the waves are rolling high and all seems lost, the child of God knows that this is not the end. It may be gloom now, but it will be glory later on. As the psalmist said, "Weeping may endure for a night, but joy comes in the morning" (Psalm 30:5 NKJV).

> Pressed out of measure and pressed to all length,
> Pressed so intensely it seems beyond strength.
> Pressed in the body and pressed in the soul,
> Pressed in the mind till the dark surges roll.
> Pressure by foes, pressure by friends,
> Pressure on pressure till life nearly ends.
> Blessed pressure, pressed into knowing no helper but God.
> Pressed into loving the staff and the rod.
> Pressed into liberty where nothing clings,
> Pressed into faith for impossible things.
> Pressed into living a life in the Lord,
> Pressed into living a Christ life outpoured.[1]

That is what testing will do for the child of God!

There is a crown of life for those who stand the test of

life. Now, don't misunderstand: this is not the crown of eternal life, which is the gift of God through faith in Christ. You don't work for that crown of salvation, and a believer can never lose it, either. But God has also promised that He will give a crown of life as a reward to those who will stand the test, and through the experience, learn to love Him:

> *Do not fear any of those things which you are about to suffer. Indeed, the devil is about to throw some of you into prison, that you may be tested, and you will have tribulation ten days. Be faithful until death, and I will give you the crown of life.* (Revelation 2:10 NKJV)

A believer cannot lose his salvation, but there is a danger of losing the crown of reward:

> *Behold, I am coming quickly! Hold fast what you have, that no one may take your crown.* (Revelation 3:11 NKJV)

God tests us, my beloved, for a definite purpose. It's not meaningless or senseless. Testing will either drive you to the Lord, or it will drive you away from Him. So many Christians become bitter. My friend, it is not going to be a pleasant experience to come someday into the presence of Christ if you have let the very thing your heavenly Father was using to develop your character, and bring you into a loving relationship with the Lord Jesus Christ, make you bitter. We will have testings, but there is going to be a crown of life for those who persevere under trial.

> *Testing will either drive you to the Lord, or it will drive you away from Him.*

You cannot escape suffering. Trials and troubles are going to come to you, whether you are saved or unsaved. Job said, "Yet man is born to trouble, as the sparks fly upward" (Job 5:7 NKJV). Man has nothing but trouble in this life. Two of the oldest pieces of sculpture that have come down from the ancient pagan world testify to that. The first one is the sculpture of the *Dying Gaul*. He has around his neck the torque that indicates he came from Gaul and was, therefore, a ferocious warrior. Even with his tremendous muscles, his body is defeated, and he is unable to stand up against the opposition. My friend, this world is not your friend, and it will see to it that you have trouble. The other sculpture I have in mind is that of *Laocöon and His Sons*. Because the priest Laocoön tried to warn the people of Troy about the Trojan Horse, the gods who favored the Greeks sent serpents as a curse upon him. Laocöon's two sons were entangled by the serpents, and when Laocöon attempted to save them, they all three were crushed to death. My beloved, you cannot cope with the troubles and problems of this life. They will get you every time.

There is only one who can deliver you. He says, "In the world you will have tribulation; but be of good cheer, I have overcome the world" (John 16:33 NKJV). Jesus Christ today is the answer for your troubles, for your sorrows, for your trials. You cannot bear your burdens alone, so He'll bear them for you. He'll give you a deliverance and a freedom if you come to Him. Then, when He tests you, He will prove that you are genuine. He has said, "You did not choose Me, but I chose you" (John 15:16 NKJV), so you can be sure that He will see to it that you stand the test.

TWO

JUSTIFICATION

BY WORKS

THE GENERAL ASSUMPTION AMONG believers is that James is diametrically opposed to the doctrine of Paul—that Paul says one thing and James, in turn, says the very opposite. We touched on this in the previous chapter, but there is much more to say about it. I'd like to give the Scriptures that are often used to defend this argument. For instance, Paul said:

> *Therefore we conclude that a man is justified by faith apart from the deeds* [works] *of the law.* (Romans 3:28 NKJV)

Now that seems, does it not, to contradict what James said in his epistle:

> *For as the body without the spirit is dead, so faith without works is dead also.* (James 2:26 NKJV)

Then we turn again to Paul:

> *Just as Abraham "believed God, and it was accounted*
> *to him for righteousness."* (Galatians 3:6 NKJV)

We seem to have a contradiction when we compare that to James' words:

> *Was not Abraham our father justified by works when*
> *he offered Isaac his son on the altar?* (James 2:21 NKJV)

Then, if we believe that Paul wrote Hebrews, we find that he said:

> *By faith the harlot Rahab did not perish with those*
> *who did not believe, when she had received the spies*
> *with peace.* (Hebrews 11:31 NKJV)

And yet James said:

> *Likewise, was not Rahab the harlot also justified by*
> *works when she received the messengers and sent them*
> *out another way?* (James 2:25 NKJV)

By just a surface comparison of these verses, it would seem that Paul put the emphasis upon faith, James put an emphasis upon works, and that the two contradict one another. The skeptic points to these and says they prove that there are contradictions in the Bible. But, of course, the answer to the skeptics is that there is no contradiction in God's Word. The contradiction is in the thinking of man and not in the written Word of God. As I've already contended, Paul and James were discussing the same subject. Allow me to repeat that faith is the theme of the Epistle of James. Nowhere did James say that works without faith is the way to get saved. He didn't even indicate that works can contribute to anyone's salvation at all. This is a very important lesson that we as believers should understand, and I hope that by the time we've concluded, you will see that these two great apostles were saying the same thing.

INTERPRETATION OF FAITH

We need a definition of faith that's in the context of Scripture—one that will help us to see precisely that Paul and James were in perfect agreement in what they said, and that they were, in fact, discussing the same subject but from different viewpoints. Someone has pointed out that Paul and James do not stand face-to-face, fighting against each other, but back-to-back, fighting the same foe. Both of them, my friend, defend the citadel of faith. To see that clearly, we need to understand the terminology that these two men used.

When Paul spoke of faith, he was talking about *saving* faith—a faith that is genuine and real and that transforms a man's life. It is a faith that brings about a revolution, as it did in his life—the kind of faith that allowed him as an old man to write: "But what things were gain to me, these I have counted loss for Christ" (Philippians 3:7 NKJV). When Paul became saved, he changed his entire book-keeping system! He stopped trusting in works and instead put his faith in Jesus Christ as the only one who could save him.

> Paul's salvation by faith *led him* to work *as he had never worked before.*

But Paul's salvation by *faith* led him to *work* as he had never worked before. Had he not come to Christ, he probably would never have left the borders of Palestine. But when he came to Christ, Paul went as a missionary throughout the world. May I say to you, when Paul came to Christ, his faith had a transforming effect on him. And when he spoke of faith, he was referring to *saving* faith.

Now, James, when he talked about faith, was referring to *professing* faith. The Amplified version really brings out James' meaning:

What is the use (profit), my brethren, for anyone to pro-
fess to have faith if he has no [good] works [to show for it]?
Can [such] faith save [his soul]? (James 2:14 AMPLIFIED)

He spoke not of real faith, but of professing faith—that which is phony and counterfeit. I believe the gravest danger that we who preach the gospel face is being willing to accept an impudent nod of the head or a brazen and flippant "yes" as evidence for saving faith when people are asked to accept Christ. Just saying "Yes, I'll accept Him" doesn't save anyone.

The story is told that Satan called a meeting of all his demons and said to them, "The purpose of this meeting is to come up with ideas for wrecking God's work down there in the world. Who has a suggestion?" One demon got up and said, "I think we ought to persuade men that there is no God. If we can do that, we'll wreck His work." But Satan said, "Look here, even *we* believe there's a God. And man does have a certain degree of intelligence, so it would be pretty hard for us to pull that off."

Then another demon called out, "We ought to try and persuade men that Jesus Christ never really existed or lived, but that He was merely a fiction, and the facts that they tell concerning Him didn't happen at all." Satan replied, "Well, that sounds good, and there will be clever intellectuals who will come along and do a pretty good job of pushing that philosophy, but even they won't succeed. Because, after all, once you've attempted to make a myth out of the Scripture, you still have a person by the name of Jesus Christ on your hands, and what are you going to do with Him? So we had better not use that tactic."

Then some other demon got up and said, "Let's suggest to men that death ends it all—that there's nothing beyond this life, and they ought not to worry about anything after death." But Satan said, "If we could convince man of that, it would be clever. But the problem is that man would think God was a fool to create mankind without having a future in mind for them. Then some of them would be apt to think that through and come to the conclusion that man has been created for eternity."

Then the wisest demon, who had not said anything up to that point, stood up and said, "I tell you what I think we ought to do. We should tell everybody that God and Jesus Christ do exist. We'll even tell them that they ought to believe in Him and that He can save them. But then we'll add that all they need to do is profess faith in Him, and then they can go on living in sin." That is how the Christian faith is being destroyed today—by those who profess faith in Christ but do not really have saving faith at all.

Paul said the same thing:

> *By which also you are saved, if you hold fast that word which I preached to you—unless you believed in vain.*
> (1 Corinthians 15:2 NKJV)

The word "vain" used here is not the word that is typically used in the New Testament. It actually means this: "unless you have just made a profession of faith." In other words, Paul said, "You're saved if you keep in memory what I've preached to you. Unless you just made a profession of faith in Christ, in which case it was not real to begin with."

Don't you see that Paul and James were saying the same thing? These two men were in perfect harmony in their discussion on faith.

Now, what about works? When Paul spoke of works, he was referring to the works of the law, and the Mosaic Law in particular. Notice these Scriptures:

Therefore by the deeds [the works] *of the law no flesh will be justified in His sight, for by the law is the knowledge of sin.* (Romans 3:20 NKJV)

Therefore we conclude that a man is justified by faith apart from the deeds [the works] *of the law.* (Romans 3:28 NKJV)

But that no one is justified by the law in the sight of God is evident, for "the just shall live by faith." (Galatians 3:11 NKJV)

Part of Paul's theme was: "No law can save a man." James agreed with him on that, and his epistle says the same thing. James made it clear that the works of the law can't save you:

> *For whoever shall keep the whole law, and yet stumble in one point, he is guilty of all.* (James 2:10 NKJV)

We all stand before God as lawbreakers, so we are never really saved by keeping the law.

But when James discussed works, he was not referring to the works of the Mosaic Law but the works of the faith. That is, the works that faith produces—the actions that follow faith in Christ. For James said, "If there are no works to follow faith in Christ, it was merely a profession of faith" (see James 2:14).

Now the question is, did Paul agree with that? I can assure you that Paul did agree. Here is our evidence:

> *For in Christ Jesus neither circumcision nor uncircumcision avails anything, but faith working through love.* (Galatians 5:6 NKJV)

So Paul said the same thing that James said: saving faith will *work*, and if it doesn't, then it's not saving faith. Saving faith is alive; professing faith is dead.

> *For as the body without the spirit is dead, so faith without works is dead also.* (James 2:26 NKJV)

I say this kindly, but our churches today are filled with spiritual zombies: members who are nothing but dead bodies. They go through the motions of being a Christian—making genuflections, nodding their heads, and putting up their hands—but they're nothing in the world but zombies! Because, my beloved, saving faith produces works. Professing faith alone is as dead as a corpse.

A girl asked her Sunday school teacher, "How can I be a Christian and still have my way?" A great many people are having their own way and at the same time profess to be Christians. On the authority of James and Paul and the Lord Jesus Himself, I say that those folks are phonies.

For those who live according to the flesh set their minds on [obey] *the things of the flesh, but those who live according to the Spirit,* [they obey] *the things of the Spirit.* (Romans 8:5 NKJV)

My friend, if you are saved, you don't do as *you* please; you do as *Christ* pleases. A Christian's actions please Christ, otherwise, he's not a Christian. We can put it like that, because the Word of God puts it that way.

So Paul and James both said that the works of the law never lead to salvation, but that saving faith leads to good works. On some mission fields, I'm told, believers are tested before they are received into the church. But we do not do that in our home churches. All one has to do is nod his head, and we accept it. We don't make anyone produce fruit to demonstrate he's a real child of God, yet that's the interpretation that both James and Paul gave to faith.

IDENTIFICATION OF FAITH

It's my contention that saving faith can be recognized and identified by certain spiritual fingerprints. In other words, genuine faith can be verified. James gave this illustration:

> *Saving faith can be recognized and identified by certain spiritual fingerprints.*

> *If a brother or sister is naked and destitute of daily food, and one of you says to them, "Depart in peace, be warmed and filled," but you do not give them the things which are needed for the body, what does it profit?* (James 2:15–16 NKJV)

That's pretty strong, don't you think? Now, I'm trying to keep Paul and James together, and so far they're sticking close. I think you'll find they stay together right here as well, because Paul said the same thing:

Owe no one anything except to love one another, for he who loves another has fulfilled the law. (Romans 13:8 NKJV)

Therefore, as we have opportunity, let us do good to all, especially to those who are of the household of faith. (Galatians 6:10 NKJV)

Even the Lord Jesus said:

By this all will know that you are My disciples, if you have love for one another. (John 13:35 NKJV)

Then when John wrote his epistle, he reiterated Christ's point:

But whoever has this world's goods, and sees his brother in need, and shuts up his heart from him, how does the love of God abide in him? My little children, let us not love in word or in tongue, but in deed and in truth. (1 John 3:17–18 NKJV)

This does not mean we ought to give to every bum who asks for money to buy a cup of coffee when he actually intends to buy wine. I made the mistake of giving a meal to a man who said he was hungry, and I think it almost choked him to eat it because he was already so full. He really wanted money, and I found out afterward that he was nothing in the world but a deadbeat.

Years ago in the Midwest, a man knocked on the door of a farmer's house late in the evening and asked the farmer to put him up for the night, saying, "You're a Christian, I understand. So you ought to entertain strangers, since some have entertained angels unawares." The farmer looked at him for a moment and then said, "You know, I don't believe that any angel would have the smell of liquor on his breath." I'm not sure we're called upon to give blindly to anyone who claims to be in need. But I do know this, my beloved: saving faith manifests itself in a real way.

For that reason, we are given the story of Zacchaeus. When our Lord went into Zacchaeus' home, God's Word gives us no transcription of the interview that took place between them; it doesn't give us a confession of faith on the part of Zacchaeus at all, so we have to guess at it. But the minute that Zacchaeus—who was one of the biggest rascals in the Bible—exited that house, he said, "I give half of my goods to the poor; and if I have taken anything from anyone by false accusation [and he had—he was a thief, a publican], I restore fourfold" (Luke 19:8 NKJV). May I say to you, my beloved, I know something happened to Zacchaeus in that house, and I know it was saving faith by his works. As James said, faith *has* to work if it's saving faith.

James drew this conclusion from the illustration:

> ***Thus also faith by itself, if it does not have works, is dead*** [destitute of power]. ***But someone will say, "You have faith, and I have*** [good] ***works." Show me your faith without your*** [good] ***works, and I will show you my faith by my*** [good] ***works.*** (James 2:17–18 NKJV)

That's tremendous. Whereas Paul talked about the root of faith, which saves, James was talking about the *fruit* of faith. Paul also addressed the fruit of faith, but he used a little different language: "But the fruit of the Spirit is love, joy, peace, longsuffering . . ." and so forth (see Galatians 5:22–23). Even the Lord Jesus said, "I am the vine, you are the branches" (John 15:5 NKJV) and "Every branch in Me that does not bear fruit He [the Father] takes away; and every branch that bears fruit He prunes, that it may bear more fruit" (John 15:2 NKJV). His ultimate goal is that you might bring forth *much* fruit (that is, the fruit of the Holy Spirit) in your heart and life.

There is a grave danger today of professing faith and having no works to prove it is genuine. A man went to his saved friend and professed conversion. His friend asked if he'd united with a church, but his reply was, "No, the dying thief on the cross never united with a church, and he went to heaven." His friend asked if he'd observed the Lord's

> *There is a grave danger today of professing faith and having no works to prove it is genuine.*

Table. The man answered, "Oh, no. The dying thief never did sit at the Lord's Table, and he was accepted." So his friend asked if he'd been baptized, but the man said, "No, the dying thief was never baptized, and he made it." And in response to the friend's question about giving to missions, the man said, "The dying thief never gave to missions." At that point, the friend got just a little weary and said, "Well, the only difference I can see between you and him is that he was a dying thief and you are a living thief."

It's so easy to sing, "Were the whole realm of nature mine, / That were a present far too small"[1] and then drop in only a few dollars when the offering plate is passed for missions. It's easy to sing, "O for a thousand tongues to sing / My great Redeemer's praise"[2] and then use the very tongue we have to cut people down instead of attempting to lead them to the Lord. John Calvin used to say that faith alone saves, but the faith that saves is not alone. Saving faith produces a life to back it up, and all of

Scripture says that if it doesn't produce a life, it was not saving faith to begin with. It was merely professing faith.

THE ILLUSTRATION OF FAITH

James gave us two illustrations of faith, and the first was Abraham.

> *Was not Abraham our father justified by works when he offered Isaac his son on the altar? Do you see that faith was working together with his works, and by works faith was made perfect? And the Scripture was fulfilled which says, "Abraham believed God, and it was accounted to him for righteousness." And he was called the friend of God. You see then that a man is justified by works, and not by faith only.* (James 2:21–24 NKJV)

Was Abraham justified when he offered his son, Isaac? The first question to ask is: *did* he offer Isaac? The answer is no, he didn't. Then what was Abraham's work of faith? How did works save him? His faith caused him to lift that knife, intending to do a thing that he did not believe God would ever ask him to do. But since God had asked him, he was willing to do it, believing that God would raise Isaac from the dead. Abraham never actually offered Isaac, because God provided a substitute, but he would have done it if God had not stopped him. This is a choice illustration of the fact that you demonstrate your faith by your actions. The action (work) of this man was that *he believed God.*

I consider the master stroke of James to be his choice for the second illustration. Notice this:

> *Likewise, was not Rahab the harlot also justified by works when she received the messengers and sent them out another way?* (James 2:25 NKJV)

Of all the people for him to have picked! To begin with, Rahab was a Gentile—an abominable Canaanite. And then, she was a woman, and back then women didn't even count in the genealogies. (Although Rahab did get into the genealogy of Christ.) Also, she was a harlot, so that's three strikes against her. What a woman! Earlier I mentioned that Paul said of her, "By faith the harlot Rahab did not perish with those who did not believe, when she had received the spies with peace" (Hebrews 11:31 NKJV). Yet James said she was "justified by works." My first reaction is, "Why don't you boys get together and decide whether she was justified by faith or by works?" But, my friend, they both were accurate and true.

Let's look at the story of Rahab briefly:

> *Now before they lay down, she came up to them on the roof, and said to the men: "I know that the LORD has*

given you the land, that the terror of you has fallen on us, and that all the inhabitants of the land are faint-hearted because of you. [All of them believed, you see, but nobody went over to Israel's side but Rahab.] *For we have heard how the LORD dried up the water of the Red Sea for you when you came out of Egypt, and what you did to the two kings of the Amorites who were on the other side of the Jordan, Sihon and Og, whom you utterly destroyed. And as soon as we heard these things, our hearts melted; neither did there remain any more courage in anyone because of you, for the LORD your God, He is God in heaven above and on earth beneath.*" (Joshua 2:8–11 NKJV)

How was Rahab justified by works? She received the Israelite spies, concealed them from her own people, then told them how to escape without being detected. That woman living there in the city of Jericho jeopardized her life by turning her back on her old life and her own people. What was gain to her became loss. She did not say to the Israelite spies, "I'll just stand on the sidelines when you enter the city and say, 'Praise God.'" Instead, she said to them, "I'm going to *do* something. I will hide you, because I believe God is going to give the people of Israel this land." My friend, she believed God, and then she *became involved.* She was justified before

God by her faith; however, before her own people and before the Israelites, she was justified by her works.

Many years ago I went to a nursery and bought a bare root labeled "Santa Rosa plum tree." It wasn't even as big as a broom handle, and it looked no more alive than one, either. I was told to put it in the ground in a certain way, which I did. I watched it, and the next spring it began to shoot out leaves. After three years, there were blossoms on it, and then there was fruit. Do you know what kind of fruit was on that tree? Plums, because the root of the tree was a plum root.

> *If you have a genuine and living and saving faith, there is going to be fruit in your life.*

Faith is the root, and the root produces the same kind of fruit. If you have a genuine and living and saving faith, there is going to be fruit in your life. May I very kindly say to you, the Lord Jesus, Paul, and James all agree: if you really are saved, it's going to show. Paul said, "Examine yourselves as to whether you are in the faith. Test yourselves" (2 Corinthians 13:5 NKJV). Believing leads to behaving; and if you don't behave, you're not saved.

THREE

TRANSLATING BOOK LEARNING INTO LIFE

THIS IS THE DAY OF NEW TRANS-
lations of the Bible. They are coming off
the press fast and furious. I have not counted them, but I'm
confident that I have at least fifteen different translations in
my study at home. Many of these are worthy efforts to trans-
fer the meaning of the original into the English language.
Others can be labeled only loose interpretations of the original text.

In spite of the epidemic of new translations, there is a
desperate and dire need for still another translation. And
that translation must be different from the New King James
or the Authorized or the American Standard Version. It
must be superior to all of the modern efforts that are out
today.

It's possible for any Christian living to make this translation. Perhaps you are thinking, *I am not capable. To begin
with, I'm not familiar with the original text or language. And,
even if I were, I would not know which of the current manuscripts*

available would be the proper one to use! But, my beloved, in spite of these limitations, it's still possible for you to make the best translation of Scripture that has ever been made. The name of your version will be The Doer's Translation, and the basis for it comes from the Epistle of James:

> *But be doers of the word, and not hearers only, deceiving yourselves. For if anyone is a hearer of the word and not a doer, he is like a man observing his natural face in a mirror; for he observes himself, goes away, and immediately forgets what kind of man he was. But he who looks into the perfect law of liberty and continues in it, and is not a forgetful hearer but a doer of the work, this one will be blessed in what he does.* (James 1:22–25 NKJV)

Paul expressed the identical idea in just a little different package:

> *You are our epistle written in our hearts, known and read by all men; clearly you are an epistle of Christ, ministered by us, written not with ink but by the Spirit of the living God, not on tablets of stone but on tablets of flesh, that is, of the heart.* (2 Corinthians 3:2–3 NKJV)

The world may not be reading the Bible, but they are reading you and me. Someone has expressed it poetically:

The Gospel is written a chapter a day,

By deeds that you do and words that you say.

Men read what you say, whether faithless or true,

Say, what is the Gospel according to you?[1]

THE DEMANDS OF THE WORD

There is an element about the Word of God that makes it different from all other books. There are many books that can be read to gain information, knowledge, intellectual stimulation, spiritual inspiration, amusement, or entertainment. But the Word of God is different, and this is probably the reason it is not as popular as other books: it *demands action.* "But be *doers* of the word, and not hearers only" (James 1:22 NKJV). It requires attention. The Lord Jesus said, "If anyone wills to *do* His will, he shall know concerning the doctrine, whether it is from God or whether I speak on My own authority" (John 7:17 NKJV, emphasis added). Do you know why a great many people doubt the Word of God? It's simply because they've never tried it out. Jesus said that if you will *do* His will, then you'll *know.* But the Word demands that you take action: "Oh, *taste* and see that the LORD is good" (Psalm 34:8 NKJV, emphasis added).

You can read history, but it asks nothing of you. You can read literature, and although it may have a lesson to teach, there are no imperatives, no declarations, and no explanations.

> *The Word of God is a command. It is a trumpet, an appeal for action.*

You can read science, but it makes no demands on you whatsoever. You can read a recipe in a cookbook, but it does not say you have to cook. There is no demand that you mix up a batch of biscuits or bake a chocolate cake. But, my beloved, the Word of God is a command. It is a trumpet, an appeal for action. The Lord Jesus said:

He who believes in the Son has everlasting life; and he who does not believe the Son shall not see life, but the wrath of God abides on him. (John 3:36 NKJV) .

You don't find that in the writings of this world! Only in the Word of God do you find the imperatives: repent, come, believe, taste, eat, drink. This is the language of the Word of God.

All advertising today is high-pressured. Television, radio, billboards, magazines, and newspapers throw everything at the consumer. They all use the hard sell, telling you that if you do not buy a certain make of car, you won't be happy. In fact, if you believe what they say, you can make your entire family happy just by getting a new car. And if you want to increase your circle of friends, there's a certain deodorant you ought to be using. But nowhere in any of this advertising will you find that you are going to die in your sins if you don't come to Jesus Christ! Advertising doesn't tell the truth today, but the Word of God does. And it makes a demand upon you. Talk about pressure!

A successful and prominent businessman visited a church, and after the service he approached the pastor and said to him, "You made quite an impression in the pulpit. You have a very fine voice, and your sermon was well thought out. You must have spent a great deal of time in preparation and prayer. But if you were one of my salesmen, I'd fire you." The preacher was startled, of course, and asked the businessman why he felt that way. He replied, "Because you didn't ask anybody to *do* anything. You didn't get them to sign on the dotted line." Friend, the Bible that I read always asks men to sign on the dotted line.

> *Friend, the Bible that I read always asks men to sign on the dotted line.*

I believe that the greatest failure of the Christian church in recent years has been at this point. After World War II, the Western world came out of the bomb shelters and went to church—prompted by fear of the bombs, and not by fear of God. Church membership and attendance soared to new heights. I am very thankful I had a ministry during that period. I had a full church, and it was to me a glorious, wonderful time for ministry. But at that same time, lawlessness and immorality increased dramatically. Drunkenness, divorce, and juvenile delinquency escalated. And in the lives of Christians, there was a total breakdown in separation from the things of the world. What had happened? We never got the Word of God out of the passive voice and into the active voice. We never got out of the subjunctive mood and into the imperative mood. We forgot that a leather-bound Bible needs some shoe leather to go with it. It's wonderful to memorize Scripture, but the important thing is to make it mobile. Put it on wheels, and let it go somewhere.

When James said, "But be doers of the word," he did not use the ordinary Greek verb for "be," which is *eimi*. The word he used instead is *ginesthe*, which literally means "to become, to be born, to come into existence." The imperative given here is for the born-again child of God; it is not for the unsaved. God does not ask the unsaved person to do anything except believe. When the people came to the Lord Jesus and asked, "What shall we do that we may work the works of God?" He replied, "Do? Why, this is the work of God, that you *believe* in Him whom He sent." (See John 6:28–29.)

There was a man who wasn't home very often because he traveled a great deal in his business. But in spite of that, he had a big family. One night his wife had a meeting at church, so he stayed at home to watch the children. When it came time for him to put the children to bed, the little four-year-old wouldn't go. The young fellow had something he wanted to say, but it was time for bed, and that man just wouldn't hear it. So he wrestled that little one, got him into the bed, and then stayed right with him until he went off to sleep.

When his wife came home and asked how he'd gotten along with taking care of the children, he said, "I did fine—all except for that little four-year-old one." She said, "We don't have a four-year-old." He said, "Oh yes, we do. He's up there in bed." So they both rushed upstairs, approached the bed, and looked down into the peaceful yet tear-stained face of the neighbor child who lived down the street. May I say to you, God never puts the neighbor's children to bed. He doesn't ask anything of you until you become His child. But to those of us who are His children, He says, "Be doers of the word, and not hearers only."

Being a doer does not mean falling into a habit or ritual. James was not talking about doing something monotonous or routine. The intent of the Word is to produce action leading to productive performance, exciting living, and a thrilling experience! That's the kind of doer James talked

> *The intent of the Word is to produce action leading to productive performance, exciting living, and a thrilling experience!*

about. It wasn't the drab existence that a great many fundamentalists try to live. If there's one thing that the church needs today, it's creative people who have ideas. Hollywood and the business world have them, so why can't the church? God wants *creative* action, *original* thinking. Oh, to dedicate our hearts and our lives and our thinking to something new and wonderful for God! We need to be motivated by that inner desire for Spirit-filled living. If we have that motivation, then studying the Word of God will be thrilling to us.

If you are a child of God, being a hearer of His Word will lead to doing. The word James chose for "hearer" makes a distinction between being a student and an auditor. An auditor is one who comes to class, listens, but takes no examinations. He makes no preparation, he turns in no papers, he does not study, and he gets no diploma. All an auditor does is listen.

I used to have quite a few folks who would audit my

classes when I was teaching at the Bible Institute of Los Angeles many years ago. I had more trouble with the auditors than I ever did with the students. They were constantly telling me I was too hard on the students. I once had an auditor come in while I was taking the class through a review in preparation for an exam. Frankly, I was attempting to frighten the daylights out of them so that they would study. That auditor wrote me a card that read: "Shame on you for the way you are treating God's little lambs." I read that card to the class, and they found it hilarious. So I said aloud, "For the benefit of that auditor, this class is not a bunch of little lambs. They're a bunch of billy goats!"

May I say to you, I wish that after each sermon, the members of the church could be given an examination. Because there is a difference between just being an auditor and being one who hears with the idea that what he is hearing, he is going to translate into life and put into action. There are a great many folks today who have never translated into life the grace of God. But that is the exact thing James meant for believers to do when he admonished us to not be hearers only.

If we aren't translating the Word into our lives, then we are deceiving ourselves. We are engaging in self-deception. I find that Christians can rationalize their conduct better than any group of people in existence. It is very easy to fall into the trap of rationalizing our sin and our inaction.

THE DANGER OF THE WORD

Reading on in this passage by James, we discover that there is a danger in the Word of God:

> *For if anyone is a hearer of the word and not a doer, he*
> *is like a man observing his natural face in a mirror.*
> (James 1:23 NKJV)

Someone may be tempted to ask, "Shouldn't he have said 'woman'?" I confess that I have wondered the same thing. After all, women usually carry little mirrors around with them to check their hair and makeup. But then I went with my wife to a department store, and I got tired of shopping, so I sat down by the elevator while she continued. Next to me was a big mirror, and I watched those who came by. I give you my word, more men looked in that mirror than women. So I think James was rather accurate in not singling out the ladies.

A mirror is used here as a picture of the Word of God. When you look into a mirror, you see a reflection of your-self—you see yourself as you really are, your "natural face." But what does that mean in the context of the mirror's rep-resenting the Word of God? It is the face of your birth. When the child of God picks up His Word, it acts as a mirror, show-ing him the man he was when he first came to Christ. When you read the Word of God, you see the face you were born again with. Some of us really need to see that face.

The Lord Jesus said to the church at Ephesus, "Nevertheless I have this against you, that you have left your first [best] love" (Revelation 2:4 NKJV). They hadn't quite departed from that love, but they were on the way. So Jesus said to them in effect, "You are getting away from those days when you first came to Me. How sweet it was when you were first converted! How zealous you were in those days. But now you are becoming cold and indifferent." Then He offered a solution, and the Epistle of James agrees with it: "Remember the Word of God, and go back to it. Remember from where you have fallen and repent" (see Revelation 2:5). Repent means to turn around and go back. Remember, repent, and go back to where you began. There are many of us who need to do that. We need to get back to those days when we were first converted and things were so wonderful to us.

The danger, though, is of looking into the mirror, seeing the flaw, but doing nothing about it:

> **For he observes himself, goes away, and immediately forgets what kind of man he was.** (James 1:24 NKJV)

Earlier, in verse 19 (NKJV), James wrote, "Be swift to hear, slow to speak." The meaning there is to give all your attention and be alert to the Word of God. The thought of verse 24 is the same: "Don't be so quick and hasty as you look in that mirror (the Word). Don't treat it casually." A man who is just a hearer of the Word and not a doer has knowledge of the Bible, but it doesn't lead to action. He's looked in the mirror, but then he chooses to do nothing about what he sees there.

People who do not like to read in the Bible about the fact that they are sinners simply pass over those sections. That is the reason, I think, that textual preaching is out-moded. I feel that we need to go through the entire Word of God and not pull out nice, sweet verses here and there. God did not give His Word in verses; verses are man-made. We need to take the Word of God as it is.

The Word is a mirror that reveals what is wrong with you. A man who goes to the doctor and has an X-ray taken that reveals a cancer in his body can respond by saying, "I don't put much confidence in X-rays. I think I'll just ignore it and forget it." I've known some people who have said that, and they have died. When the doctor told me that I had can-cer, I wanted treatment just as quickly as I could get it. My friend, you cannot afford to read the Word of God and not respond to it. It demands your response; and if you don't respond, *you* are responsible. If the doctor tells you that you have cancer and you don't do anything about it, is the doc-tor responsible? Absolutely not. God has given you His Word, and you are responsible for your response to it. To a man who has been born again, the Word will say, "Look, you are no longer growing. You are actually leaving your first love." God uses His Word to remind us of Himself and to call us back.

I heard a song leader say that we sing "Standing on the Promises" when all we are really doing is sitting on the premises. That is what James told us not to do. The Word of God is a mirror that reveals our shortcomings, and we are not to ignore what it says.

God has given you His Word, and you are responsible for your response to it.

The Word reveals us as we are, penetrating below the surface of our beings. The Bible is not a popular book today, because it shows us who we are.

For the word of God is living and powerful, and sharper than any two-edged sword, piercing even to the division of soul and spirit, and of joints and marrow, and is a discerner of the thoughts and intents of the heart. (Hebrews 4:12 NKJV)

Out in the hills of Tennessee, there was an old mountaineer who didn't have much contact with the modern world. A group of campers went up there, and after they'd left, this mountaineer went to look around the area where they had camped. He found several things they had left behind, including a mirror. He had never seen a mirror before, so he looked into it and said, "I never knew my pappy had his picture took!" He was very sentimental about it, of course, and he took it home. He slipped into the cabin, climbed up into the loft, and hid the mirror. His wife saw him do it but didn't say anything. After he went out of the house, she went up to see what he had hidden. She found the mirror, and when she looked into it, she said, "So that's the old hag he's been running around with!"

May I say to you, it is so easy to read the Word of God and think it is a picture of someone else. But when you look into God's Word, you don't see your old pappy. You see your old nature, that old hag inside that needs to come into the presence of a Savior and be made a child of God! That's the reason many Christians today will not study the Word of God. They look into it and do not like what they see.

THE DESIGN OF THE WORD

There is a grand design in the Word of God. James said:

> But he who looks into the perfect law of liberty and continues in it, and is not a forgetful hearer but a doer of

the work, this one will be blessed in what he does.
(James 1:25 NKJV)

Those words are so rich and wonderful! You see, the idea inherent in James' use of this word "look" is that the mirror has to be low to the ground; it is down where you have to stoop to look into it. You have to have a humble mind, and there must be confession. Dr. F. B. Meyer said years ago that he'd always thought that God's gifts were put on shelves, and that as we grew taller we'd be able to get at the best gifts. But he soon came to find out that wasn't true at all. Instead of putting the best gifts on the higher shelves, God keeps them on the lower shelves. So if you want to get His best gifts, you've really got to humble yourself and get down low. And when you get down there, you're to look penetratingly and attentively.

> *If you want to get His best gifts, you've really got to humble yourself . . .*

What are you looking at? James said we're to look at "the perfect law of liberty." Let me clarify that: in his epistle, James never referred to the Mosaic Law. When he talked about law, it was the law that grace imposes on us.

Perhaps you didn't know that, but it's true: grace imposes law. You see, in the Old Testament, there is love in law. In the New Testament, there is law in love. Our Lord said, "Therefore if the Son makes you free, you shall be free indeed" (John 8:36 NKJV), but He also said, "If you love Me, keep My commandments" (John 14:15 NKJV). And then Paul wrote to the Galatians, "Bear one another's burdens, and so fulfill the law of Christ" (Galatians 6:2 NKJV). What law? Christ's law. John said in his first epistle, "For this is the love of God, that we keep His commandments" (1 John 5:3 NKJV).

May I illustrate? When you drive down a freeway, that freeway is loaded with laws. You cannot go one hundred yards without encountering a sign that reads *Turn Off, Slow Down, Enter,* or *Do Not Enter.* I've never seen a place that has as many rules and regulations as a *free*way! (By the way, you ought to see one of our southern California freeways at around five o'clock on a weekday evening. It will really make you wonder who is free.) When you're driving along and come to a sign that reads *Do Not Enter,* my friend, you'd better not enter! The freedom is to be on the *right side* of the freeway.

I once got turned around while trying to navigate the freeway system and somehow found myself on the side heading north when I wanted to be going west. But I followed the signs, "the rules," and not only did I get headed in the correct direction, I discovered a quicker route to get to my destination. I was glad for those rules, and there was a lot of freedom when I followed them.

My beloved, there is a lot of freedom in Christ. In fact, the only true liberty there is today is in Him.

I offer another illustration: There was a drunkard who was gloriously saved. One day he walked over to the repair shop to pick up his wife's sewing machine. As he was carrying it home to her, he passed by the tavern that he had often frequented before he was saved. The bartender saw him and said, "Jim, come on in here, and have a drink on me. It'll give you strength." But he replied, "No, thank you. If you really want to know the truth, there was a time when I could not carry a twenty-five-cent piece by your place. But today I can carry a machine for my wife." May I say to you, that's the kind of freedom that believers have in Christ.

If you are in Christ, you are going to obey Him—and His laws are not hard; they are not rigorous. Laws are for the weak, the natural man. Laws are for lawbreakers; honest citizens do not need the law. I do not know one-half of the laws of this state in which I live, but every shyster lawyer knows them, because he is constantly seeking loopholes to justify his clients who break those laws. But just because you are a child of God, your freedom does not entitle you to break the Ten Commandments.

Today God has called His children to a higher level. A child of God has a spiritual spontaneity, a high and lofty motive, an inspiration of God. The believer has no desire to murder. He lives above the law. He is now motivated by the love of the Savior, and he desires to obey Him.

The more we read and study God's Word, the more we'll learn, we'll love, and we'll live. Joy will fill and flood the soul. We'll not be like a galley slave, whipped and chained to his bench. We'll serve Him because, my beloved, the Word of God is having its way in our lives. It's being translated into life.

FOUR

THE ONE SUBJECT NOT TAUGHT IN GOD'S UNIVERSITY

A S WE'VE ALREADY SEEN IN THE preceding chapters, God tests His own children to prove they are genuine and reveal the reality of their faith. He weeds out the counterfeit, the phony, and the pseudo-saint. God's testing is a regular obstacle course. He uses extreme measures—both physical and mental—in testing His children. He sends suffering, adversity, disappointment, betrayal, injustice, heartbreak, and tragedy. These are all tests and trials in God's University. And then, for those whose faith proves to be real, the testing gives them an assurance that they are His children and opens up a polychrome vista of high and holy anticipation for their future.

But there is one test that God never gives. In fact, it is not in His curriculum at all. God *never* tests men with evil or with sin.

Let no one say when he is tempted, "I am tempted by God"; for God cannot be tempted by evil, nor does He Himself tempt anyone. (James 1:13 NKJV)

This is made very clear: God never tests men with evil or with any sinful pursuit.

DON'T BLAME GOD

The natural propensity of mankind is to blame God for our own fumbles, foibles, faults, failures, filth, and fall. We blame God; it's been that way from the very beginning. When sin entered the Garden of Eden, the very first thing Adam said was "The woman whom You gave to be with me, she gave me of the tree, and I ate" (Genesis 3:12 NKJV). In other words, "I'm not to blame, *she* is. And if You hadn't given her to me, I wouldn't be in this mess!" The woman passed the buck also. She said, "The serpent deceived me" (Genesis 3:13 NKJV). Neither one of them wanted to take any responsibility at all. But, actually, all three—the man, the woman, and the serpent—were responsible.

As believers, we often hear questions like "Why does God send floods and earthquakes?" May I say, that is a lame attempt to blame God. Is God responsible for floods? He may send the rain and snow, but He's also given man the intelligence to know that he ought not to build so close to the rivers and oceans! But man—through greed and selfishness and for the love of money and of pleasure—builds too close to the water, and then when the water gets too close to *him*, he calls it a flood. But God never calls it a flood. It is actually the greed and avarice of man that causes him to build where it is not safe.

Likewise, if you want to live in southern California, you're taking a chance on having an earthquake. The seismologists predict that we are in for a big earthquake here, yet people are still streaming into the area and putting up high-rise buildings. We ought not to blame God if a slab of concrete falls off one of those buildings and kills one of our loved ones. It would be much safer in the wide open spaces of Texas. I'm a Texan, but who wants to go back there? I know it's nicer there now than when I was just a boy growing up, but I want to stay here in California. However, I'm not going to blame God when the earthquake comes. We have already been warned that it is coming.

Men also blame God in their philosophies. Pantheism, which is one of the oldest philosophies, says that everything is God, and "Good is God's right hand, evil is God's left hand." But, my friend, God is neither a "rightist" nor a "leftist," and you can't blame Him for the evil. Fatalism says that everything in this world is running by blind necessity. They blame God by saying, "If there is a God at all, He has wound up this universe like a clock and gone off and left it." Materialism lays the blame on God by arguing that the loftiest aspirations and the vilest passions are the natural metabolism of a physical organism.

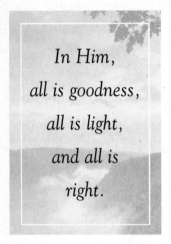

*In Him,
all is goodness,
all is light,
and all is
right.*

God has answered these philosophies in His Word. There is no evil in God, "for God cannot be tempted by evil." In Him, all is goodness, all is light, and all is right. John wrote in his first epistle, "This is the message which we have heard from Him and declare to you, that God is light [that is, He is holy] and in Him is no darkness at all" (1 John 1:5 NKJV).

WHY WAS JESUS TESTED?

Let me introduce something theological: *Jesus could not sin.* The Lord Jesus made this very interesting statement: "The ruler of this world is coming, and he has nothing in Me" (John 14:30 NKJV). Someone will immediately ask, "Why, then, was He tempted?" In Matthew 4:7, our Lord said to Satan, "It is written again, 'You shall not tempt the LORD your God'" (NKJV). The reason He was tempted was to *prove* that there was no sin in Him. After Christ had lived a life down here for thirty-three years, Satan came to Him with a temptation that appealed to man's total personality—the physical side, the mental side, and the spiritual side. The Lord Jesus could not fall, and the testing was given to demonstrate that. If it were a possibility that He could have fallen, then our salvation would be in doubt, because the minute He yielded to sin, we would have no Savior.

Let me illustrate this with a very homely story from my boyhood in West Texas. My dad built cotton gins for the Murray Gin Company, and we lived in a little town that was near a branch of the Brazos River. In the summertime, there wasn't enough water in that river to rust a shingle nail, but when it began to rain in the wintertime, you could almost float a battleship on it. One year, a heavy flood washed out the wooden bridge on which the Santa Fe railroad crossed the river. They replaced it with a steel bridge, and when they'd completed it, they brought in two locomotives, stopped them on top of the bridge, and tied down both of

> *Jesus was tested to prove that you and I have a Savior who could not sin.*

the whistles. All of us who lived in that little town knew for sure that something was happening. We ran down to see what it was—all twenty-three of us! When we got there, one of the braver citizens asked the engineer, "What are you doing?" The engineer replied, "We're testing this bridge." The man asked, "Why? Do you think it's going to fall down?" That engineer drew himself up to his full height and said, "Of course not! We are *proving* it won't fall down." For the same reason, Jesus was tested to prove that you and I have a Savior who could not sin.

TEMPTED BY SIN

God doesn't want to tempt you with evil, my friend; He wants to save you *from* it! So He never uses sin as a test.

However, God does permit us to be tempted with sin, and David is a good example of that.

> **Again the anger of the LORD was aroused against Israel, and He moved David against them to say, "Go, number Israel and Judah."** (2 Samuel 24:1 NKJV)

That was a sin. In fact, it was the greatest sin David ever committed. But did *God* tempt David with evil? My friend, to understand the Bible, you always need to get the full story. In 2 Samuel, you have man's viewpoint of the recorded events. From man's viewpoint, it looked as if God was angry with Israel, and He simply had David do this. However, in 1 Chronicles we are told God's viewpoint:

> **Now Satan stood up against Israel, and moved David to number Israel.** (1 Chronicles 21:1 NKJV)

Who provoked David to sin? It was Satan, not God. God merely permitted Satan to do it because He was angry with Israel and its sin. God never tempts men with evil.

WHO IS RESPONSIBLE FOR SIN?

Who, then, is responsible for our propensity for evil? What causes us to sin? Perhaps you're thinking now, *McGee, you've just said that Satan causes it!* And that is what the average Christian believes today. But that is Satan's lie, if you please. Notice what God's Word says:

> **But each one is tempted when he is drawn away by his own desires and enticed.** (James 1:14 NKJV)

Who's to blame for your sins when you are drawn away to do evil? God is not to blame for your sin. The devil is not responsible. Do you know who is responsible? *You* are.

A man got lost in the hills of Arkansas back in the days

of the Model T Ford. He had lost his way, and there were no highway markings. He came into a small town and saw some little boys playing there. He asked one of them, "Where am I?" The little fellow looked at him, puzzled, for just a moment. Then he pointed at the man and said, "*There* you are!" My friend, when you ask, "Who tempted me to do this?" God says, "*There* you are." It's in your own skin—that is where the problem is.

Notice that James said, "*Each one* is tempted." That is a declaration of the individuality of the personality of the human race. Just as each one of us has a different finger-print, each one of us has a different moral nature. We have our own idiosyncrasies, our own eccentricities.

Two men were talking, and the first one said, "Everybody has some peculiarity." But the second gentleman disagreed and argued that he didn't have any. So the first man said, "Well, then, let me ask you a question. Do you stir your coffee with your right hand or with your left?" His friend answered, "I stir it with my right hand," and the first man exclaimed, "Well, that's your peculiarity. Most people stir their coffee with a spoon!"

May I say to you, all of us have our peculiarities. Many things are not bad within themselves, but it is the use we make of them that is wrong. Food is good, but you can become a glutton. Alcohol is medicine, but you can become an alcoholic if you abuse it. Sex is good if it is exercised within marriage. When it is corrupted by the evil heart of man and exercised outside of marriage, then it is sin. One person may be tempted to drink. Another may be tempted to overeat. Another may be tempted in the realm of sex. And as far as God's Word is concerned, there is no difference. The problem is always within the individual. No outside thing or influence can make us sin. The trouble is within us, in that old nature that we have.

Many psychologists are trying to help us get rid of our guilt complexes. A Christian psychologist once told me, "You need to emphasize in your teaching that guilt complex more than you do. A guilt complex is as much a part of you as your right arm. You just cannot get rid of it." The godless psychologist, on the other hand, attempts to remove it in the wrong way. For example, a Christian lady I knew was told by a psychologist that her problem was that she was too religious, and that what she needed to do was go down to the barroom and pick up the first man she could find. Then there are other psychologists who say, "What about your background? Did your mother love you? Did anything unusual happen while you were in the womb?" If you said, "Well, my mother was caught in a rainstorm while she was carrying me," the psychologist would say, "That's the reason you're a drip!"

There are a lot of Christians who are trying to blame somebody else for their difficulties and problems. Our trouble is on the inside, so we can't point the finger at anybody else. Shakespeare had it right: "The fault . . . is not in our stars, / But in ourselves, that we are underlings."[1] Our problem is within us.

My beloved, what we need is to go to the foot of the cross. You could solve a great deal of your problems for which you are blaming someone else if you would say to the living Lord Jesus, who is right now at God's right hand, "I'm a sinner. I'm guilty." Then He will remove your guilt complex—He is the only one who can do that.

> *He will remove your guilt complex—He is the only one who can do that.*

Solomon said, "For as he [man] thinks in his heart, so is he" (Proverbs 23:7 NKJV). The solicitation to sin always must have a corresponding response from within. James said that it is by our own desires that we are "drawn away" into sin (James 1:14 NKJV). Our Lord Jesus used the same word, "draw," when He said, "I . . . will draw all peoples to Myself" (John 12:32 NKJV). But the scoffer comes along and says, "Preacher, you are wrong. He doesn't draw *me* to Him at all." My friend, He doesn't force you. Hosea tells us that He will use only "bands of love" to draw us to Himself (Hosea 11:4 NKJV). He wants to woo and win you by His grace and love. If you don't respond to that, it's your fault and not His.

THE CONCEPTION OF SIN

Frankly, evil is attractive today; it is winsome. Man can be enticed; the hook can be baited. James put it like this:

> *Then, when desire has conceived, it gives birth to sin; and sin, when it is full-grown, brings forth death.*
> (James 1:15 NKJV)

Let me give you my translation: "When the desire of the soul, having conceived, gives birth to sin, the sin, having been completed, brings forth death."

James used an interesting word here: "When desire has *conceived.*" Conception is always the joining and the union of two, so the desire of the soul has been joined with something else. What has it been joined with? Here is where good men disagree. Some think it is the devil. Do you know what it is, in my humble judgment? It is the desire of the soul joined to the outward temptation. When you bring those two together, sin is conceived. The Lord Jesus said in the Sermon on the Mount that if you are angry at your brother, you are guilty of murder (see Matthew 5:21–22).

What begins in the heart moves out into action and becomes sin. He also said that if you so much as look upon a woman with the thought of committing adultery with her, you are already guilty of it (see Matthew 5:28). Why? Because sin always begins in the heart.

The natural question at this point is this: is temptation sin? The answer to that is *no*. Temptation is not sin. Martin Luther used to say that you can't keep the birds from flying over your head, but you can keep them from building a nest in your hair. To be tempted is no sin. For there to be sin, a conception must take place with the thought in the heart and action carried out on the outside. Sin is the consummation of the act, inwardly and outwardly.

What did James mean when he said that sin "brings forth death"? There are three kinds of death spoken of in Scripture. There is *physical* death, and that comes to every man, you can be sure of that. Then there is *spiritual* death, which is the condition of the lost man—he is "dead in trespasses and sins" (Ephesians 2:1 NKJV). Finally, there is *eternal* death, which is the fate of the man who dies an unbeliever. The word "death" in James 1:15 means primarily *separation*. Therefore, for a believer it means that when sin is born in his life, when it becomes an action, his fellowship with God is broken. There is a separation. If you are a child of God, sin immediately breaks your fellowship with Him—

and that is death, by the way. In 1 John 1:6 (NKJV) we read, "If we say that we have fellowship with Him, and walk in darkness, we lie and do not practice the truth." You cannot have fellowship with Him and permit sin continually to happen in your life.

James said:

Do not be deceived, my beloved brethren. (James 1:16 NKJV)

Here, "deceived" means "to wander, to roam about, or to stray." It is like the little lost sheep that the shepherd went out after. James was saying, "Don't wander. Don't think that somehow you can get by with sin." The habitual and perpetual sinner definitely does not have a line of communication with God; he never has been born again. If you can live in sin and enjoy it, you are not a child of God—it's just that simple.

The story is told of the Calvinist and the Arminian who were having an argument. The Calvinist believes that once you are saved, you can never be lost; the Arminian believes you can lose your salvation. The Arminian said, "If I believed your doctrine and was sure I was converted, I would take my fill of sin," to which the Calvinist replied, "How much sin do you think it would take to fill a genuine

Christian to his own satisfaction?" May I say to you, that is a tremendous answer. If you can be satisfied with sin, you need to examine yourself to see whether or not you are in the faith at all to begin with.

My friend, all of us are subject to temptation, but let's make sure that we do not give birth to sin. There can be no abortion here if you go through with temptation. Sin and death *will* be the end result.

Man calls sin an accident; God calls it an abomination.

Man calls sin a blunder; God calls it blindness.

Man calls sin a chance; God calls it a choice.

Man calls sin a defect; God calls it a disease.

Man calls sin an error; God calls it enmity.

Man calls sin an infirmity; God calls it iniquity.

Man calls sin fascination; God calls it a fatality.

Man calls sin a luxury; God calls it leprosy.

Man calls sin a liberty; God calls it lawlessness.

Man calls sin a trifle; God calls it a tragedy.

Man calls sin a mistake; God calls it madness.

Man calls it a weakness; God calls it willfulness.

There is within you and me that which could take us to hell today. The only one who can deliver us is Jesus Christ, the sinless one. He will not tempt you with sin, but He will deliver you from it.

Come to Me, all you who labor and are heavy laden [with a burden of sin]*, and I will give you rest.* (Matthew 11:28 NKJV)

FIVE

FREEDOM OF SPEECH
IN GOD'S UNIVERSITY

THE CHURCH TODAY HAS A PROBLEM concerning freedom of speech. It's called gossip, and every Christian has a problem with it. The Word of God has more to say about the use and abuse of the tongue than it does about the use of alcohol or any other thing that we think of as a sin.

James, as dean of God's University, considered this a controversial subject, and he gave considerable space to it. In fact, he took up the topic right at the very beginning of his epistle. It appears that he couldn't wait to get to this subject, and he emphasized it a great deal.

So then, my beloved brethren, let every man be swift to hear, slow to speak, slow to wrath. (James 1:19 NKJV)

Not only was James a great educator, as we've seen in this epistle already, but he actually was an ear and throat spe-

Have you ever noticed that God gave all of us two ears and only one tongue? That in itself is a message, isn't it?

cialist. He dealt with the use of the ears and the use of the tongue, or the throat, if you please.

Have you ever noticed that God gave all of us two ears and only one tongue? That in itself is a message, isn't it? Someone may ask, "Why did He give us two ears?" Well, the main reason is that most of what we hear goes in one ear and out the other; one receives it, and the other lets it out. But God gave us only one tongue, which means that we are to listen twice as much as we talk. And have you ever noticed that our Creator put the tongue in a cage? Assuming you don't take your teeth out at night, God has put your tongue in a cage, and many times we need to grit our teeth and keep that little animal—the most dangerous animal there is—in the cage where it belongs. Charles H. Spurgeon wrote:

"The boneless tongue, so small and weak,
can crush and kill," declared the Greek.

"The tongue destroys a greater horde,"

    the Turk asserts, "than does the sword."

A Persian proverb wisely saith,

    "A lengthy tongue—an early death;"

Or sometimes takes this form instead,

    "Don't let your tongue cut off your head."

"The tongue can speak a word whose speed,"

    the Chinese say, "outstrips the steed;"

While Arab sages this impart:

    "The tongue's great storehouse is the heart."

From Hebrew wit this maxim sprung,

    "Though feet should slip, ne'er let the tongue."

The sacred writer crowns the whole,

    "Who keeps his tongue doth keep his soul!"[1]

Someone has said that a fool's tongue is always long enough to cut his throat, and another that tongues run faster when they have little to carry. Someone else has said that it takes a baby two years to learn to talk and fifty years to learn to keep his mouth shut.

I have another: An old bachelor met an old maid, and they started going together. He'd never gotten married, because he always felt women talked too much. But this woman did not talk, and he was very much smitten by her, so he proposed. Well, that just set her off. She started talking, and she talked for about two hours straight. Finally, she

> The tongue is the most dangerous weapon in the world. It's more deadly than any bomb.

noticed that he hadn't said anything, so she asked him, "Sam, why don't you say something?" He said, "I've said too much already."

The tongue is the most dangerous weapon in the world. It's more deadly than any bomb. There is today much talk about international weapons inspections, but what we really need is an inspection of the tongue. When I first came to the pastorate at the Church of the Open Door, someone sent me a little card printed with these words: "In Balaam's day it was a miracle when an ass spoke; it's a miracle today when one keeps quiet." I do not think whoever sent that meant anything personal by it, but it offered a sound piece of advice.

Because the tongue is so dangerous, James addressed the issue immediately by saying that we are to be "swift to hear, slow to speak, slow to wrath." He didn't wait long to add:

If anyone among you thinks he is religious, and does not

> **bridle his tongue but deceives his own heart, this one's**
> **religion is useless.** (James 1:26 NKJV)

If a religious man does not control his speech, his religion is in vain. That is harsh. Yet James had more to say about it in chapter 3:

> **Indeed, we put bits in horses' mouths that they may**
> **obey us, and we turn their whole body.** (James 3:3 NKJV)

David said, "I will guard my ways, lest I sin with my tongue; I will restrain my mouth with a muzzle [bridle], while the wicked are before me" (Psalm 39:1 NKJV). In other words, because he wanted to give the right kind of testimony, David would put a bridle in his mouth. My friend, there are a lot of Christians today who ought to have bridles put in their mouths.

Bridle bits are not impressive in size, but they can hold a high-spirited horse in check and keep him from running away. If you are old enough, you may have recollections of the horse-and-buggy days. I can recall seeing a horse run away, turn over a buggy, and bring death and destruction to a family. In the same way, the tongue can run away. Someone said of another individual, "His mind starts his tongue to wagging and then goes off and leaves it." We should not go through life like that—we need a bridle for the tongue.

Then James used a different illustration:

Look also at ships: although they are so large and are driven by fierce winds, they are turned by a very small rudder wherever the pilot desires. Even so the tongue is a little member and boasts great things. (James 3:4–5 NKJV)

Large ships can be controlled by a little rudder, which few people even see. A fierce storm may drive a ship, but a little rudder can control it. Likewise, the tongue can also steer us and change the course of our lives. Men have been ruined by the tongue, and many the fair name of a woman has been wrecked by some gossipy tongue.

If you read chapter 3 through, you'll find that James used many figures of speech to speak of the tongue. But notice this:

For every kind of beast and bird, of reptile and creature of the sea, is tamed and has been tamed by mankind. But no man can tame the tongue. It is an unruly evil, full of deadly poison. (James 3:7–8 NKJV)

If you've ever been to the circus, you know that people can tame great big elephants and teach them to stand on their hind legs, and they can train lions and tigers and leopards to work in the same cage. But James said that the little tongue cannot be trained. That's one animal that no zoo has in captivity, no circus can make perform, and no man can tame.

I once sat in a restaurant and overheard the conversation of two women sitting in the booth next to me. In the span of about fifteen minutes, they absolutely destroyed the reputations of at least half a dozen men and women. Their tongues were, without doubt, the most dangerous things imaginable. If a man had whipped out a gun and held up the cashier at the restaurant, there would have been a headline in the paper. But nothing was said about those two tongues—even though they did more damage than any machine gun could possibly have done. May I say, that is true in our churches as well; our tongues hurt the church more than anything else.

Now, the tongue can also be a wonderful instrument, of course. Solomon wrote in Proverbs:

> *A word fitly spoken is like apples of gold in settings of silver.* (Proverbs 25:11 NKJV)

> *A man has joy by the answer of his mouth, and a word spoken in due season, how good it is!* (Proverbs 15:23 NKJV)

The tongue is what lifts us above the inarticulate animal world. We are not gibbering apes or aping parrots. We can

Our tongues give us away.

put thoughts into words and use them to express ourselves. It is also our ability to communicate by the use of the tongue that lifts mankind to the highest level.

The tongue is also our badge of identification. It is the index, the table of contents, of our lives. It is the fraternity pin that we wear, revealing our character. In other words, our tongues give us away.

Because of the broad reach of my radio program, and the fact that I have an unusual accent, I have had some very interesting encounters that illustrate this point. Years ago, I traveled to Portland, Oregon, to speak at a conference. A group of pastors were all staying at the same motel, and one evening before the service, we went over to the restaurant across the street. We were having a lot of fun talking like a bunch of students who were "out of school." Across from us sat two women. One of the preachers nudged me and said, "Those women are listening to us." I cut my eye around, and I could tell that they were indeed listening. They looked to be very nice ladies, and I couldn't imagine their eavesdropping on a conversation.

They finished their meal and left, so we thought nothing more of it. But when we went back to the motel, those two women were standing in front of the office. We started to pass, and one of them said, "Dr. McGee, is that you?" After I'd replied in the affirmative, she said to her friend, "I told you so!" Then they explained that they'd recognized me in the restaurant. I asked, "Have you met me before?" They had not. So I asked if they'd ever visited the church where I pastored. The one lady said she had never been to my church, but the second lady said, "I've been there, but I always sit back in the balcony. So I've never seen you close up or really known just how you look. But the minute I heard your voice, I knew who you were."

May I say to you, your voice gives you away. Your tongue tells who you are. You just can't escape that. I would even argue that your voice is the best identification that you have. I think it's even better than a fingerprint, because it tells your character; it reveals who you really are.

God is listening to you, and He is listening to me. He heard that whispered conspiracy. He heard that word of slander. He heard that falsehood. He heard that cutting remark. He heard every obscene utterance that you have ever given, as well as that foul blasphemy. He heard you, and that told Him who you are. "For out of the abundance of the heart the mouth speaks" (Matthew 12:34 NKJV).

I wonder, would you be willing to have a tape played of everything you have said this past week? Suppose someone had secretly recorded everything you said—would you want to hear it? I don't think I would. But I'll say this: if we could listen to everything we've said this past week, we'd know whether or not we are Christians, wouldn't we? Have you this week used your tongue in such a way that people would know you are a child of God? The tongue is a dead giveaway. It tells who you are, where you came from, whether you are ignorant or educated, cultured or crude, clean or unclean, vulgar or refined. It tells whether you are a believer or a blasphemer, a Christian or a non-Christian, guilty or not guilty. Do you want that tape played?

The writer of the Book of Proverbs said:

Death and life are in the power of the tongue. (Proverbs 18:21 NKJV)

Think of that! Your tongue can be used to give out the gospel, and that will give life. It can also be used to say things that would drive people away from God forever, which makes it an instrument of death. It's no wonder that David said, "I'm going to be very careful of what I say when I'm in the presence of the wicked, because I do not want to disgrace God. I do not want to turn them from God" (see Psalm 39:1). David also put it like this:

Do not be like the horse or like the mule, which have no understanding, which must be harnessed with bit and bridle, else they will not come near you. (Psalm 32:9 NKJV)

Oh, my beloved, the tragedy is that, with your tongue, you can send somebody else either to heaven or to hell.

It is interesting to note that Paul said you're saved when your heart and mouth are brought into conformity in the confession of faith:

That if you confess with your mouth the Lord Jesus and believe in your heart that God has raised Him from the dead, you will be saved. (Romans 10:9 NKJV)

Many hold the viewpoint that Paul here was referring to public confession, but that is incorrect. What it does mean is that if you believe in your heart that God raised Jesus Christ from the dead and can bring your mouth into conformity with your heart and say, "I believe that Jesus Christ died for my sins, and if I trust Him, He'll save me"—then you are saved. It's amazing. The tongue can send you to heaven or send you to hell; it's a ticket in both directions.

So what about freedom of speech in the University of God? Dean James said, "Shut up." That's a sign they ought to put up in our churches. During my pastorate, we had a nice, polite little note that we put in the bulletin for the morning service that read: "Let the first note of the organ bring worshipful silence." James said, "Keep quiet. Bring that tongue into obedience of Jesus Christ. Be still and know that He is God."

You know, it's wonderful sometimes to be quiet and find out that God is God. There are too many of us who talk too much. A great many people say, "Oh, we should witness more." That is true, but what we really should do is keep our mouths shut more. More people have been turned away from Christ by listening to Christians than by anything else.

God has given you the most wonderful gift in the world: the gift of speaking. Isn't it tragic if you choose to take that glorious gift and blaspheme your Maker, or turn people away from God, when you could use that tongue to confess the glories of your Savior? We don't need to sing "O for a thousand tongues to sing" if we'd just use the one we've got for His glory. We need to have a tongue that is controlled by the Spirit of God, because—though no man can control the it—God is an animal trainer, and He can tame your tongue.

GOD'S WAR ON
POVERTY AND RICHES

HOW ARE WE TO TREAT PEOPLE in the different strata of society—the rich, the poor, the middle class? God has a war on poverty and riches, but His war on poverty is a little different from that of our government. No matter which political party has been in office, neither the federal nor the state governments have been able to deal successfully with this problem. The fact of the matter is, part of the curse on the human race is poverty and riches. The most difficult people to reach are those who are the most poverty-stricken and those who are the richest; it seems to be almost impossible to reach either class with the Word of God.

The real problem is actually the imbalance of wealth. The wealth of the world is in the hands of a few, while the bulk of the population can be classified as poor. The fact of the matter is, you and I do not know what real poverty is. There are people in some parts of the world who have never known what it is to have a full stomach. There is great famine in parts of India and Africa, for example. Contrast that to the luxury and abundance of the wealthy.

God goes after this problem in the Epistle of James, and I am very delighted to say that He is on the side of the poor. After all, when the Lord Jesus came into the world, He wasn't a rich man's boy. He wasn't born with a silver spoon in His mouth. He was born in poverty in a borrowed stable. He had to borrow loaves and fishes from a little lad to feed the crowd. He also spoke from a borrowed boat, and He never did have a place of His own to lay His head (see Matthew 8:20). He had to borrow a coin to illustrate a truth, and then He borrowed a donkey to ride into Jerusalem to present Himself as the Messiah. He borrowed a room to celebrate the Passover, and then He died on a borrowed cross—it belonged to Barabbas, not to Him. Not only did it belong to Barabbas, but to you and me, because it was for our sin that He was put there. And then, they put Him in a borrowed tomb—it belonged to Joseph of Arimathaea. So when the Lord Jesus Christ came down to this earth, He knew what poverty really was. It was part of the curse that He bore.

When I was in college, a preacher came and talked about "the blessings of poverty." Now, I was a poor boy, and I mean *poor*, my friend. I was going to school on borrowed money and was working full time. That man spoke every morning in chapel, and I was told that he got fifteen thousand dollars a year. That was back in the days when a dollar was worth a dollar, so it was a lot of money for a preacher at that time. You know, what he had to say just ran off my mind like water off a duck's back—he had no message for me. The blessings of poverty? I just happen to know, since I was born that way and haven't gotten too far from it yet, that there are no blessings in poverty. Poverty is a curse, and it was part of the curse that Christ bore.

Riches can also be a curse, as James showed in his epistle. Paul said, "For the love of money is a root of all kinds of

> *Poverty is a curse, and it was part of the curse that Christ bore.*

evil" (1 Timothy 6:10 NKJV). Paul and James certainly agreed here. You can spend your money on the wrong items, and you can deposit your money in the wrong bank. "Do not lay up for yourselves treasures on earth, where moth and rust destroy and where thieves break in and steal" (Matthew 6:19 NKJV). All the banks are telling us where to put our money, but God says in effect, "I've got a bank, and I will keep investments up there for you." I'm a literalist as far as the Bible is concerned, and I actually believe that you can take money and so use it down here that it's put in the bank of heaven up yonder for you, my beloved; I believe that it's put into the legal tender of heaven.

Our Lord watched a poor widow bring a few little mites and drop them into the treasury. Those mites didn't amount to much when compared to the wealth of the temple of Herod; whether she gave or not didn't help or hurt the work of that temple at all. But our Lord took her few little coppers, and He kissed them into the coin of heaven. (See Mark 12:41–44.) I believe that wealth down here on earth can be used for the glory of God. It's not the amount, if you please, but it is the way that it is used for God.

James had a great many harsh things to say to rich people. For example:

> *But you have dishonored* [despised] *the poor man. Do not the rich oppress you and drag you into the courts?* (James 2:6 NKJV)

> *Come now, you rich, weep and howl for your miseries that are coming upon you! Your riches are corrupted, and your garments are moth-eaten. Your gold and silver are corroded, and their corrosion will be a witness against you and will eat your flesh like fire. You have heaped up treasure in the last days.* (James 5:1–3 NKJV)

He was speaking about those who have made their life's endeavor just to accumulate money down here for no other purpose than to have it and not to use it for the glory of God. I overheard two Christian men talking about a third Christian, and their comment was quite interesting. One of them said, "You know, the way that he is after money, you'd think he's intending to take it with him!" I'm afraid there are a great many Christians who are so involved in making money that it has become their entire goal in life. I've always prayed that God would not let me go to either extreme. "Give me neither poverty nor riches" (Proverbs 30:8 NKJV). In the middle of the road is the preferred place to go through life.

But what is God's solution to the problem of poverty? It is not to rob the rich in order to take care of the indigent, the lazy, the indolent, the drones, the loafers, the sluggards, and the laggards. On the other hand, God would never destroy the dignity, self-respect, integrity, and

> God would never destroy the dignity, self-respect, integrity, and honor of the poor by placing them on charity.

honor of the poor by placing them on charity. God's war on poverty and riches does not march under the banner of the dollar, where millions are appropriated for relief. And it is not aimed primarily at the head or at the stomach, but at the heart. It is a war against class distinctions and divisions in the church that mar the body of Christ.

I prefer the Amplified translation here; I find it does a better job than I do in translating James:

> *My brethren, pay no servile regard to people [show no prejudice, no partiality]. Do not [attempt to] hold [and] practice the faith of our Lord Jesus Christ [the Lord] of glory [together with snobbery]!* (James 2:1 AMPLIFIED)

What James was saying is simply this: don't profess faith in Christ, and at the same time, be a spiritual snob; don't form cliques in your church. *All* believers are brethren in the body of Christ, whatever their status or denomination. There is a fellowship of believers, and friendship should be over them as a banner.

Now James addressed the total community of believers, and in his day it was a cosmopolitan group. There were the rich, the poor, the influential, the common people, the high and the low, the slave and the free, the Jew and the Gentile, the Greek and the barbarian, the male and the female. My beloved, we are all in the body of Christ, and nationality and color and class have nothing to do with it. When you're in Christ, you're *one* in Christ. We need to emphasize that in these days. There is a brotherhood within the body of believers, and the Lord Jesus Christ is the common denominator. Friendship and fellowship are the legal tender among believers.

James said not to hold your faith with respect of persons. If you belong to the Lord Jesus Christ, and another person belongs to the Lord Jesus Christ, he is your brother. Furthermore, if a sinner comes into your assembly, or you otherwise come into contact with him, remember that he is a human being for whom Christ died. He stands at the foot of the cross, just as you do.

The Old Testament taught Israel not to regard the person of the rich or of the poor. God, in the Mosaic system, cautioned:

> *You shall do no injustice in judgment. You shall not be partial to the poor, nor honor the person of the mighty. In righteousness you shall judge your neighbor.*
> (Leviticus 19:15 NKJV)

Simon Peter learned this lesson at Joppa when God let down from heaven the sheet full of unclean animals and commanded him to eat of them. Peter concluded from that experience, "In truth I perceive that God shows no partial-ity" (Acts 10:34 NKJV).

James was very practical and down-to-earth. The fact of the matter is, I know of no epistle that pinches like the Epistle of James. He hurts us, because he gets right down to where we are living—or, probably, I should say where we're *not* living.

He used a stinging illustration to make his point:

For if a person comes into your congregation whose hands are adorned with gold rings and who is wearing splendid apparel, and also a poor [man] in shabby clothes comes in, and you pay special attention to the one who wears the splendid clothes and say to him, Sit here in this preferable seat! while you tell the poor [man], Stand there! or, Sit there on the floor at my feet!
(James 2:2–3 AMPLIFIED)

The way James described this rich man is quite interesting. James mentioned that he wore gold rings. This has caused misunderstanding among a great many saints, and there are actually some who won't even wear a gold ring, saying that Christians shouldn't. But that is nonsense, for James was not saying that at all. Actually, the literal is this: "There comes into your assembly a gold-ringed man." You have to put yourself back in that day. Men who moved in the upper echelons wore rings to distinguish themselves from the common people, who wore no rings at all. And the more rings, the better. Our translation also says "splendid apparel," but the literal is "bright and shining clothes." That rich man was really ostentatious, overdressed, and pretentious. He made his entrance into the church with his flags flying, a fanfare of trumpets, parade and pageant, and strutting like a peacock. The minute that man stepped in and flashed his rings around, the usher said, "My, here's a very rich man. We'd better give him the best seat in the place!" I think James saw that happen in some church and gave us this illustration from real life, because he didn't like it at all. Therefore, he remarked about it.

In contrast, the poor man came in with tattered and torn clothing. It may have been clean, but there was evidence of patches and poverty. He may even have been shabby and shoddy, dilapidated and deteriorated. James placed these two men in contrast—each at an extreme end of the social ladder.

I heard a story years ago about a very spiritual man who always wore frayed garments to church, and people began to criticize him. Especially, there was one lady who would judge him. But one afternoon she went over to his home and found out that he had a paralyzed wife, and he was spending all of his money taking care of her. May I say to you, that woman quit criticizing him. We do not know why certain people dress a certain way, and we have no business judging them because of it.

Now, in James' illustration, that poor man entered and the usher said, "You take the seat back here." In our day, this would be like putting the poor man way back where the ushers sit or telling him to stand up in the rear. In that day, there were a few seats down front where only the prominent people were allowed to sit. In the United States, there was a day when we had paid pews in our churches. They had little doors to them, and only the family who had paid for that pew could sit there on Sunday. You couldn't sit with whomever you wanted to sit. Today we have our little cliques that take a certain section in a church, and woe to the stranger (especially if he is not well dressed) who comes in and sits next to that crowd! I can assure you he will get a cold shoulder.

We don't see too many of these extremes between the rich and poor in this relatively affluent country today. In the early days of my ministry, our congregation had extremes; there were the well-dressed people, and then there were those who were poor and not well dressed. But in most of our churches today, just about everyone looks as if he's doing alright. We don't have that distinction that we once had. But there were people in those days who would say to me, "Well, Dr. McGee, we'd like to come to church, but we don't have nice clothes." Have you ever met folks like that? Some of us older folks may be able to remember back to days like that. I can remember that as a boy, I used to complain to my dad that I didn't want to go to Sunday school because I had patches on my pants, and I didn't want to wear them on Sunday. But he just warmed up those patches and sent me on! And I went, let me tell you! But I didn't want to do it.

After James had put these two men in contrast, he asked:

Are you not discriminating among your own and becoming critics and judges with wrong motives? Listen, my beloved brethren: Has not God chosen those who are poor in the eyes of the world to be rich in faith and in their position as believers and to inherit the kingdom which He has promised to those who love Him? (James 2:4–5 AMPLIFIED)

That is quite wonderful. What James was saying is that a believer may not be rich in money or position, and yet he may be the richest man spiritually in that church.

> A believer may not be rich in money or position, and yet he may be the richest man spiritually in that church.

The Word of God says a great deal about the poor. God has made it very clear from Genesis to Revelation that He has a concern and consideration for them. The poor never get a fair deal, and they never have. As long as men are natural men and are not born-again Christians, the poor will never get a fair deal in this world. Their only hope is in Jesus Christ. Listen to the Word of God:

> *But He saves the needy from the sword, from the mouth of the mighty, and from their hand.* (Job 5:15 NKJV)

And then in Job 36:15 we read:

> *He delivers the poor in their affliction, and opens their ears in oppression.* (NKJV)

Psalm 9:18 promises:

> *For the needy shall not always be forgotten; the expectation of the poor shall not perish forever.* (NKJV)

Also in Psalms we read:

> *Your congregation dwelt in it; You, O God, provided from Your goodness for the poor.* (Psalm 68:10 NKJV)

For the LORD hears the poor. (Psalm 69:33 NKJV)

For He will deliver the needy when he cries, the poor also, and him who has no helper. He will spare the poor and needy, and will save the souls of the needy. (Psalm 72:12–13 NKJV)

He shall regard the prayer of the destitute, and shall not despise their prayer. (Psalm 102:17 NKJV)

Scripture after Scripture speaks of the poor and of God's concern for them.

One of the most wonderful encounters with our Lord was when John, who was in prison, sent two of his disciples to our Lord, and they asked Him, "Are You the Messiah?" The Lord Jesus responded, "Go back and tell John this: the blind receive their sight, the lame walk, the lepers are cleansed, the deaf hear, and the dead are raised up. All of that was prophesied of the Messiah." But He crowned it all with this: "And the poor have the gospel preached to them." (See Matthew 11:2–5.)

God has a great deal to say about the mistreatment of the poor on this earth by the rich and those who are in power. Someday they will have to answer to Him for it. But the poor can be rich in spiritual things, and that is the important thing for the poor man to see.

> God has
> rubbed out
> all class
> distinction at
> the cross.

My beloved, God has rubbed out all class distinction at the cross. He says to the rich, "You come as a beggar to Me; you have nothing to offer. And if you are poor, you can come without money and without price. Because at the cross, I waged a successful war against poverty and against riches. I can save you, and that's the most wonderful thing I can do for you." You may not have anything to offer Him, but you can still receive from Him the gift of eternal life. He's able to save us by His mercy because of the blood that He shed for us. He doesn't care who you are—whether rich or poor, black or white, yellow or red, Jew or Gentile. He came to die for all.

SEVEN

WHEN DOING GOOD IS WRONG

SAYING THAT DOING GOOD IS wrong appears to be a contradiction of terms. After all, isn't doing good the opposite of sin? And isn't right always the opposite of wrong, and there's no way in the world of reconciling the two? I'm willing to concede that this subject is a paradox, but I'm not willing to agree that it is a contradiction.

If it is a contradiction, then our freeway system is also full of contradictions. The other day I drove down the coast of southern California on my way to San Luis Obispo. As I approached the appropriate exit, I saw a sign that said *San Luis Obispo, Next Exit*. Now I've known for years that San Luis Obispo is to the left of the freeway, and yet that off-ramp took me to the right. My friend, you can't get a greater contradiction than that. If the town is on the left-hand side and you are told to drive off to the right, doesn't that seem like a contradiction? But the minute I drove down that off-ramp, it turned, took me on an overpass, and I came out right there in San Luis Obispo. So it may have been confusing, but it was not a contradiction.

Likewise, as we approach this subject of when doing good is wrong, our confusion comes from our limited notions of sin. When most of us think of sin, we think only of personal sins, but those make up but a small portion of sin as given in the Word of God. And even in the realm of personal sins only, our thinking is confined and limited because each one of us has a peculiar notion of just what sin is. But sin is not what we *think* it is; it's what Scripture says it is.

> *Sin is not what we think it is; it's what Scripture says it is.*

WHAT IS SIN?

Let me share some scriptural definitions of sin. This is not an exhaustive list, by any means, but perhaps these passages will make things clearer.

> **Whoever commits sin also commits lawlessness, and sin is lawlessness.** (1 John 3:4 NKJV)

The breaking of the law is sin, and that is what is known as a sin of commission.

> **All unrighteousness is sin.** (1 John 5:17 NKJV)

Unrighteousness fails to meet the standard of God. It's a failure to *do*, and that's a sin of omission.

Another definition of sin is excessive talking:

> **In the multitude of words sin is not lacking, but he who restrains his lips is wise.** (Proverbs 10:19 NKJV)

I would argue that one could not listen to a conversation over a period of about an hour without somebody sinning in the use of his lips.

Then we have this from Paul:

> **But he who doubts is condemned if he eats, because he does not eat from faith; for whatever is not from faith is sin.** (Romans 14:23 NKJV)

That is, any line of conduct or any act—even if it is "good"—that is not done in the outflow of faith becomes a sin. This, by the way, should dictate Christian conduct. It is the Holy Spirit's answer to questionable things. If a believer has a question about any matter of conduct, then it is wrong.

As we've already seen, it is also a sin to have respect of persons:

> **But if you show partiality, you commit sin, and are convicted by the law as transgressors.** (James 2:9 NKJV)

> **He who despises his neighbor sins.** (Proverbs 14:21 NKJV)

Then, there is another area in which we can sin: the thought life.

> **The devising** [thought] **of foolishness is sin, and the scoffer is an abomination to men.** (Proverbs 24:9 NKJV)

No act at all, but just the thought of foolishness is sin. The writer of the Proverbs also said:

> **A haughty look, a proud heart, and the plowing of the wicked are sin.** (Proverbs 21:4 NKJV)

Pride and vanity are two things that the Word of God condemns, even more than drunkenness. But what are we to make of "the plowing of the wicked" being sin? I can't think of anything more innocent and less conducive to sin than plowing. Yet the Word of God says that when an evil man

with an evil heart does anything—even plowing—it will
not be accepted in His sight.
It is sin.

> *We have seen through these Scriptures that personal sins have two categories: one of doing and the other of not doing.*

We have seen through
these Scriptures that personal
sins have two categories: one
of doing and the other of not
doing. One is an overt act of
breaking God's law; the other
is a failure to act when we
should. The breaking of the
law is a sin of commission;
failure to do good is a sin of
omission.

That brings us to the passage in James that I'd like to
focus on:

**Therefore, to him who knows to do good and does not
do it, to him it is sin.** (James 4:17 NKJV)

Sin is not just in harming. A great many people say, "Well,
I've never harmed anyone." But have you ever failed to help
someone? May I say to you, in God's sight, that's just as
grievous a sin.

Perhaps you are familiar with that infamous night years

ago in New York City when the night air was rent asunder by the screams of a woman being murdered. Her calls for help were heard by many occupants of apartments in that neighborhood, but they did not do anything. Some of them heard but then merely turned over in their beds and went back to sleep. Several others actually opened their windows and looked out, but they did nothing. When questioned, they said, "We didn't want to become involved." All of those people, as far as we know, were law-abiding citizens, and yet that was a horrible thing that they did—they failed to act. "To him who knows to do good and does not do it, to him it is sin."

I heard of another account, also in New York, of an entire family that was involved in a terrible car accident. They were driving down the freeway when the car spun out of control, went over the embankment, and two or three members of the family were killed. The husband crawled back up to the highway and attempted to flag down a passing driver. Car after car passed by the scene, but no one was willing to stop. I heard also of an incident involving a man in Michigan who fell on the snow and broke his leg. He crawled up to a road, but he could get no one to stop. So he crept right out onto the highway! It delayed traffic because people were slowing down to pull around him, completely ignoring his attempts to tell them his condition. They did not want to become involved.

LET'S GET PERSONAL

You may be thinking, *Well, I would never neglect people in need like in those awful instances you just mentioned,* or *I don't get arrested,* or *I don't hurt anyone!* Of course you don't. That's not what James was talking about. So let's bring this right down to where we live, to our own personal lives.

You know that you ought to give more to missions, but you don't. It's sinful to know that we should do more and not do it. You know that you ought to get involved in the work of the church, but you are not doing it. May I say to you, that's sin in God's sight. You know that you ought to go to Sunday school or attend a ministry retreat or join a Bible study, but you do none of these things! May I say to you, God says that's sin.

I was once approached by a man who handed me a check made out for the amount of money he had just made in a business deal. With it was a note that read: "When I first got this money, I was going to buy myself some new fishing gear. But then I got to thinking about it. My old fishing gear is good, so I'm going to use it and give this to the radio ministry instead." May I say to you, friends, let's bring this down to where we live and put it in shoe leather. This is something that should be real to us. We know we should witness to a friend, but we've never witnessed to him. We know that we should bring a relative of ours to church, but we've never done that. According to God, that is sin.

FAILURE TO DO

The Lord gave a parable of three men who took their talents and used them in different ways. One man took that talent and buried it. He wanted to be able to return it to his master, and he ought to be commended for that, should he not? He was a good man, but his master said to him, "You wicked and lazy servant! You should have been using this! You should have been doing something with it." (See Matthew 25:26.) His sin was a failure to *do*.

> *The sin of a failure to act is greater than the overt sin of doing something.*

The sin of a failure to act is greater than the overt sin of doing something wrong. May I again illustrate this? The newspaper recorded the account of a man who brought his young family to southern California, but he couldn't get a job and his family was hungry. He got desperate and held up a liquor store. May I say to you, he was wrong. He broke the law—there is no question about that. But I have a certain sympathy for a man who has a hungry family. And I believe that in God's sight, he is less guilty than some of us who know that we ought to be doing something and yet are not doing it. No one can deny that what that fellow did was wrong, but he had mitigating circumstances. And when he went before the judge, he received a certain amount of mercy. But what about the man who knows what he should do and does not do it? May I say to you, in the sight of God, I think the man who fails to do is more guilty than the man who sometimes does that which he knows he should not do.

There are two words translated in Scripture as our English word "know." One is the word *gignosko*. It occurs many times in the Word of God, including in reference to salvation: "That you may know that you have eternal life" (1 John 5:13 NKJV). It means to know by observation or experience. It's the word that you take in the laboratory to say that you know this element is what it is because you've tested it. But the word used in James 4:17 is *eidoti*, which means to know by reflection. It's that which you turn over in your mind and know because you have reflected on it. You have certain facts, you've put them together, and you come to a certain conclusion.

Let me illustrate. You do not need to go to India today to know that last night, multitudes of people went to bed hungry. You do not know it because of observation; you haven't been there by experience. But you know it because of the information that has been brought to you. Likewise, you do not have to go out and interview everyone in your town to know that at this very moment, many people without Christ are walking into a lost eternity. In your neighborhood, in your place of business, you know there are people without Christ and without God. You know that about you today are needy people who are without Christ, without God, and without hope in this world.

I went out to the golf course with two other preachers, and a fine-looking gentleman asked in a very gracious manner if he could join us. We all agreed it would be fine, and I said, "But I think I ought to tell you something. We are three preachers, and maybe you don't want to play with preachers." But he didn't mind, so we started out. He was very much reserved at first. But after we'd played a while, and he saw that we were human beings as well as preachers; we got to calling him by his first name, and he became very close and familiar before we finished up. We were on the fifteenth hole when we sat down, and this man opened up his heart. He was a well-to-do man, but he told us about the problems he was having in his home and with his grown children. My, the burdens and problems that man had! He just opened up and talked, and before we finished, we had invited him to the service. He did come to a service, and I do not know what decision he may have made in his heart. But I do know this: around us today, friends, are many people that we could help. You know of someone whom you could speak to that no one else could reach, because that individual has confidence in *you*.

It's so easy today to shut ourselves up in our churches and let the rest of the world go by. A man once said to me that during every service he prays that people might make decisions for Christ. But I had that man in my congregation for seventeen years, and he never once brought a person with him to church. I don't think God hears prayers like that, my beloved. I think God is quite realistic. Many of us are in a Sunday school class or small group, and these can become exclusive little clubs where we shut out the world and cold-shoulder visitors.

My beloved, there is a wall running down through the churches of this land. It's the wall of silence, the wall of indifference, the wall of *doing nothing*—nothing for God!

Many of us are in a Sunday school class or small group, and these can become exclusive little clubs where we shut out the world and cold-shoulder visitors.

Doing good in the mind is sin when it goes no farther! When we retire into our ivory towers and ignore the world out there, that is sin.

John told about Judas—not Iscariot—sitting in the Upper Room, listening to those wonderful words of the Lord Jesus. He said, "Lord, how is it that You will manifest Yourself to us, and not to the world?" (John 14:22 NKJV). What about the world out there? That man—the first missionary, by the way—knew "to him who knows to do good and does not do it, to him it is sin."

As a college student, I read Joseph Conrad's wonderful book, *Lord Jim*. It tells the story of a man who failed at the crisis moment. He was an officer on a ship carrying a bunch of manual laborers out of India. One night a storm began to blow, and a great big hunk of rust broke off of the ship. The crew knew that at any moment the water would come rushing through there. So this officer, together with several others, boarded a little lifeboat and deserted the ship, which is the worst thing an officer can do. He did *nothing* at the moment when he should have been doing *something*. And the remainder of the story is that of a man, who, for the rest of his life, engaged in fool acts of bravery in an attempt to compensate for that. I believe there will be multitudes of believers in heaven whom our Lord will point His finger at and say, "You did not do this, and you did not do that. You knew that you should have done it, and you did it not."

DO SOMETHING

Faith, in the Epistle of James, is not a theory. It is not part of a make-believe world or a will-o'-the-wisp. It's a reality. James put faith in action. It works, and if it's not in action, it's not saving faith at all. Having good intentions but doing nothing is sin. Hearing a brother being maligned or misrepresented and keeping quiet, saying, "I don't want to become involved," is not any different from those people who stayed in their apartments in New York City, or those motorists who went by and saw the man lying in the snow and ice. It's not any different—it's all doing nothing. My beloved, we should *do* something.

There is another sin that falls under this: refusing to confess or correct our mistakes. Drs. Arthur T. Pierson and Louis Sperry Chafer were two great men of God. One Saturday afternoon they met in the post office, and Dr. Pierson said to Dr. Chafer, "Louis, did you hear about this?" and then he repeated an incident about a certain preacher they both knew, and the story was not very complimentary. The next morning, Sunday, Dr. Chafer got up very early, and he looked down the hill and saw Dr. Pierson in his shirtsleeves and suspenders, hitching up his horse. He was driving out that morning to preach. When Dr. Pierson finished hitching up the horse, he rode up the hill, rapped on the door of Dr. Chafer's cottage, and said, "Louis, you remember yesterday I told you such and such about So-and-so? Last night I found out that's not true. I want you to forget it; I made an awful mistake for even repeating it, even if it had been true. I ask your forgiveness."

Do you know what Dr. Pierson had been doing? He had been taking a spiritual bath that morning before he went to preach. He was cleaning the deck, cleaning up his life, and he recalled that he'd said something unkind and detrimental about a brother. My friend, he could have driven out that morning and just kept quiet and not admitted that he'd made a mistake. But that man wanted to preach that morning in the power of the Spirit, so he did something to correct himself. My friend, he knew that "to him who knows to do good and does not do it, to him it is sin."

A WORD TO THE UNSAVED

If you happen to be an unsaved person, you may be thinking, *I'm not a Christian, so I couldn't commit that sin.* May I say, if you are unsaved, you have committed the greatest sin that any person can possibly commit.

> *Nevertheless I tell you the truth. It is to your advantage that I go away; for if I do not go away, the Helper* [the Holy Spirit] *will not come to you; but if I depart, I will send Him to you. And when He has come, He will*

convict the world of sin, and of righteousness, and of judgment: of sin, because they do not believe in Me. (John 16:7–9 NKJV)

The greatest sin, the one sin that the Holy Spirit convinces and convicts of, is the sin of rejecting Jesus Christ. All you have to do to commit that sin is just do nothing about Him.

A man was drowning, and a lifeguard swam out to him and said, "I'll take you in." But the drowning man said, "Oh, no, no, no. I'm going to try and make my way back. I think I can do it." The lifeguard said, "But it looks like you are going down!" Still the man refused to allow the lifeguard to touch him. So the lifeguard said, "I risked my life to come out here and get you!" And the man said, "That's alright, I don't want your help." So the lifeguard returned to the shore and, of course, the man went down. Why did he drown? Because he couldn't swim? No. He drowned because he refused to accept the offer of help.

> *The greatest sin, the one sin that the Holy Spirit convinces and convicts of, is the sin of rejecting Jesus Christ.*

My friend, Jesus Christ left heaven's glory, came down to this earth, shed His blood, went through hell for you on that cross, was buried and raised from the dead, went back to heaven, and He's saying to you now, "I can forgive every sin under the sun except this one thing: if you continue to do nothing, if you continue to reject Me, if you continue to turn your back on Me and have nothing to do with Me, you're lost, and you will go down." That's the greatest sin that you can commit.

What must one do to be saved? "Believe on the Lord Jesus Christ, and you will be saved" (Acts 16:31 NKJV). What must one do to be lost? Nothing. Absolutely nothing!

EIGHT

TO WHOM SHOULD
WE CONFESS?

A GREAT RELIGIOUS SYSTEM operating today bases one of its tenets on this Scripture:

> *If you forgive the sins of any, they are forgiven them; if you retain the sins of any, they are retained.* (John 20:23 NKJV)

The assumption is that to man is granted the authority to forgive sins here upon this earth.

Now, the apostle Peter is purported to be the founder of this church, so let's take a moment to notice what he said about this:

> *Nor is there salvation in any other, for there is no other name under heaven given among men by which we must be saved.* (Acts 4:12 NKJV)

Him God has exalted to His right hand to be Prince and Savior, to give repentance to Israel and forgiveness of sins. (Acts 5:31 NKJV)

To clarify, what are the grounds for salvation? The apostle Peter made it very clear that there is salvation only in Jesus Christ, and that He alone can forgive sins when a sinner goes to Him directly. Then in what do we have remission of sins? Well, it's by faith in the Person of Christ that you and I have remission of sins; Scripture makes it very clear that only God can forgive sins.

> *It's by faith in the Person of Christ that you and I have remission of sins . . .*

You may remember that when the man on the stretcher was let down through the roof by four men, the Lord Jesus said to him, "Son, your sins are forgiven you" (Mark 2:5 NKJV). At that time, the scribes challenged Him, saying, "Who can forgive sins but God alone?" (Mark 2:7 NKJV). The Old Testament had taught them that only God could forgive sins, and they were right in that. Isaiah recorded these words of our God:

I, even I, am He who blots out your transgressions for My own sake; and I will not remember your sins. (Isaiah 43:25 NKJV)

Then, in Daniel's great prayer of confession, we read:

To the Lord our God belong mercy and forgiveness, though we have rebelled against Him. (Daniel 9:9 NKJV)

And Micah said:

Who is a God like You, pardoning iniquity and passing over the transgression of the remnant of His heritage? (Micah 7:18 NKJV)

And from David we have this:

I said, "I will confess my transgressions to the LORD," and You forgave the iniquity of my sin. (Psalm 32:5 NKJV)

So the scribes knew from the Old Testament that only to God were they to direct their requests for forgiveness of sins.

So when the apostle Peter said of Jesus, "For there is no other name under heaven given among men by which we must be saved," he was saying that the only thing in the world that can remit a person's sins is the death of Christ upon the cross—or the gospel. A man must hear the gospel to be saved and have his sins forgiven. That poor fellow on the stretcher would never have heard the Lord Jesus say, "Son, your sins are forgiven you," if the men carrying the stretcher hadn't brought him there. So, in one sense, they remitted his sins, because they brought him to the only physician who could heal him—the Great Physician.

But then what did it mean when our Lord said, "If you forgive the sins of any, they are forgiven them"? Well, only the gospel as it's preached to men can remit their sins. "So then faith comes by hearing, and hearing by the word of God" (Romans 10:17 NKJV). So what the Lord Jesus was say-ing was this: "I have died for you and come back from the dead. I now have given you the gospel, and believing the message contained in it about Me is the only thing that can remit men's sins. When you preach this gospel and people receive it, their sins are remitted; they're forgiven. But if you don't take it to them, my beloved, they will not hear, will not believe, and their sins will not be forgiven." The gospel, therefore, must be preached—that Christ died for our sins, was buried, and rose again the third day, according to the Scriptures.

Our Lord said to Peter and the others gathered in the Upper Room, "I will give you the keys of the kingdom of heaven" (Matthew 16:19 NKJV). What are the keys? The authority of the Scriptures! The scribes carried keys indicative of the fact that they had the key to the Word of God. But the Lord Jesus said, in essence, "I'm taking it away from the scribes, and I'm now giving it to those who are followers of Me, who believe the gospel and have trusted Me as Savior." If you're a believer in the Lord Jesus Christ, He has given that key to you as well. My friend, when you preach the gospel, or you give the gospel to someone, then you are indeed using the keys.

> *If you're a believer in the Lord Jesus Christ, He has given that key to you as well.*

Peter, like all other believers, may have been given the keys, but he never asked anyone to confess to him. On the contrary, he did the very opposite. We have a very fine illustration in his ministry when he went up to Samaria and met a fellow by the name of Simon:

> **And when Simon saw that through the laying on of the apostles' hands the Holy Spirit was given, he offered them money, saying, "Give me this power also, that anyone on whom I lay hands may receive the Holy Spirit." But Peter said to him, "Your money perish with you, because you thought that the gift of God**

could be purchased with money! You have neither part nor portion in this matter, for your heart is not right in the sight of God. Repent therefore of this your wickedness, and pray God if perhaps the thought of your heart may be forgiven you." (Acts 8:18–22 NKJV)

If there ever was an opportunity for Simon Peter to set an example of confessing to a man, here was the chance! After all, he was the first pope of the church. Why didn't he say, "Simon, come in here and confess your sin to me, and I'll forgive you"? No. He said, "Go to God, and ask Him to forgive you, for He *alone* can forgive you this sin."

> We have a gospel that can give men the remission of their sins—if it's given to them.

Paul never asked anyone to confess to him, either. You'll recall that there was sin in the church at Corinth, and Paul instructed them to deal with it. Once they had, he wrote and told them to forgive the brother who had confessed. He didn't say, "Wait until *I* get there, and let him confess to me, so that I can forgive him his sin." No, it was to the church that the brother was to confess. (See 2 Corinthians 2:5–8.)

May I say to you, we have been given the keys. We have a gospel that can give men the remission of their sins—if it's given to them. If it's not given, they'll not receive remission of sins.

I do not think we have taken the responsibility of the keys seriously enough. Billions of dollars have been spent to get to the moon; in comparison, mere pennies are spent to get the gospel to China or India or the Middle East! God has given the keys to every single believer, and yet there are multiplied numbers of people around the globe who have never heard the gospel. Thank God for the wonderful missionaries who go to the corners of the earth, but very few do. And I suspect that if we don't start doing our part, God will eventually say, "You had the keys, but you did not use them. Now I'm taking them from you as I took them from the scribes years ago." May God help us in this late hour to begin using the keys!

Another favorite verse of those who endorse confession of sins to a man is from our Epistle of James:

> **Confess your trespasses to one another, and pray for one another, that you may be healed. The effective, fervent prayer of a righteous man avails much.** (James 5:16 NKJV)

It was on the assumption and presumption of this verse that the confessional came into existence. But what did James really mean when he said, "Confess your trespasses to one another"? The word here for "confess" means, in the original Greek, "full, frank, and open confession" of sin. Then "trespasses" here is the Greek *paraptoma*, meaning "to stumble and fall down." It's the same word Paul used when he said to the Galatians:

> **Brethren, if a man is overtaken in any trespass** [if one of your brethren stumbles]**, you who are spiritual restore such a one in a spirit of gentleness, considering yourself lest you also be tempted** [because you might stumble and fall in just the same way that brother did]. (Galatians 6:1 NKJV)

And Paul used the same term when he addressed the Ephesians:

> **And you He made alive, who were dead in trespasses and sins.** (Ephesians 2:1 NKJV)

Trespass is a sin, but it's a special kind of sin. It's when we stumble and fall. Just as when we hurt someone by taking hold of him as we're physically falling or stumbling, sometimes we hurt the cause of Christ and the church when we trespass.

So to whom are we to confess? We confess sins to God!

But we confess faults—these stumblings—to the ones we've hurt, to one another. "Confess your trespasses [faults] to one another." If I hurt you, I should confess to you. If you hurt someone else, you should confess to him.

Notice that James said "to one another," not to one man. My beloved, no believer is above another believer. When I started out in the ministry as an ordained Presbyterian preacher, I wore a Prince Albert coat and a winged collar. I wish you could have seen me—I looked like a mule peeking over a whitewashed fence! My, how dignified I thought I was. Well, as is true with a lot of young preachers, I

Just as when we hurt someone by taking hold of him as we're physically falling or stumbling, sometimes we hurt the cause of Christ and the church when we trespass.

took a long time to learn something: before God, no one man is exalted above another. Before God, we either stand complete in Christ, or we don't stand at all. Therefore, we all are, as John said, "kings and priests" (Revelation 1:6 NKJV). Every believer is a priest; we all stand before God equal in Christ.

Friend, we need to confess our faults to each other more. I believe it would make the church a sweeter place. Fellowship, too, would be sweeter if sometimes we would admit that we are wrong. You'd be amazed how much difficulty could be erased from the church if people would just go to their brothers and sisters in Christ and say, "I'm sorry that I hurt you. I was at fault." We all make mistakes. And in order to have Christian fellowship, we should confess them. When we stumble, we should let our brother know that we did not intend to hurt him at all. Wasn't James practical?

> *We all make mistakes. And in order to have Christian fellowship, we should confess them.*

May I say, my beloved, we are to confess our faults to one another, but we're to confess our sins to God, and that's a very private matter. I've never liked for anyone to come to me and confess sin. I think that is something that ought to be directed to God. He alone can forgive you, not any man down here.

NINE

WHAT IS
WORLDLINESS?

I'VE LIKENED THE EPISTLE OF James to God's University, with James as the dean. This metaphor holds good through the entire epistle. And as we've seen, there are exams and quizzes in God's University just as in any other. The difference is that James, who is always very pragmatic, hands out the questions to study, and he even gives us the answers! We don't have to buy or steal to pass these exams. We just turn to the Epistle of James, read the questions, and get the answers. But in spite of the fact that all of this information is given out, these are hard quizzes and stiff examinations. They must be wrought out on the anvil of life. They're experiments that must be made in the laboratory of life to prove whether or not they work.

The quiz we are presented with now is: what is worldliness? As I pose that question in our "classroom," I imagine hands going up all over, because a lot of people think they know the answer. The first pupil called upon says, "It's the kind of amusements that you attend, like going to movies or dances or drinking and smoking—that's worldliness." Someone else offers, "It's the kind of a crowd you run with. After all, birds of a feather flock together." Another hand goes up, and that person argues, "No, it's the conversation that you engage in. Your conversation can be on most any subject, but you just have to weave in a 'Praise the Lord' or a 'God led me . . .' every now and then to prove that you are not a worldly Christian." Then another calls out, "You reveal whether you're a worldly Christian by the way you dress." (I once heard a woman say that the trouble with being a woman these days is that she's got to look like a girl, dress like a boy, think like a man, and work like a dog! Our dress certainly is a complicated matter, but we move on because there may be some other ideas.) Going on to the next, we have this answer: "A worldly person engages in business and the making of money to the exclusion of all else. He neglects the church." The next individual offers something that hits rather close to home. He says, "It's the person who does not go to church but spends his time on the golf course." Let's not pick only on the golfers and add to that answer those who go out fishing or boating or to the baseball stadium instead of attending church!

These are only a few of the answers, and it may be that you have something you'd like to add. But if you agree with any of these that I have mentioned, you flunked the exam.

Because I have the Epistle of James before me, I have the question that he asked, I have the answer that he gave, and none of these is right.

I hasten to say that these things we've mentioned are merely symptoms of a disease, and the disease is worldliness. I knew a man who had a sick wife, and after they'd visited the doctor, a neighbor asked him, "What did the doctor say that your wife had?" The man answered, "The doctor said my wife had one of the worst cases of symptoms he'd ever seen!" May I say to you, you may have a case of symptoms, but nobody ever died of symptoms—he dies of the disease. These are simply evidences of the real problem, which is deeper. A pastor had a clock in his church that never would keep accurate time. So he put a sign under the clock that read: "Don't blame the hands. The trouble lies deeper." This is what we need to recognize in ourselves. What we call worldliness is just the hands of the clock; the real trouble lies deeper.

Two outstanding Christians and brilliant men of the past got at the heart of the matter. One was the novelist William Thackeray, who wrote a novel called *Vanity Fair*, referring to the world. The characters in that novel are filled with weakness, littleness, meanness, pettiness, jealousy, envy, and discord. Someone once asked William Thackeray, "Why is it that your heroes are not heroes, and your heroines are not heroines?" He responded, "My business is to hold the mirror of nature up to life, and in life I see no heroes or heroines." *Vanity Fair* does not end with "They lived happily ever after." It ends like this: "Ah! Vanitas Vanitatum! which of us is happy in this world? Which of us has his desire? or, having it, is satisfied?—come, children, let us shut up the box and the puppets, for our play is played out."[1] Dr. Griffith Thomas, another great man of the past, was approached by a person who asked him if he thought the world was becoming Christian. Dr. Thomas reportedly answered, "The world is becoming just a little churchy, but the church is becoming tremendously worldly." May I say to you, those two men got at the nub and the very heart of what worldliness really is.

> The world is becoming just a little churchy, but the church is becoming tremendously worldly.

Before World War II, there was a wall of separation between the church and the world. It was a legalistic, and I believe, unscriptural wall in many respects. The church was sort of like the little Dutch boy who kept his finger in the dike to keep the water out. But then there was the aftermath of war, the entrance of television, the rise of lawlessness and immorality, existentialism, the futility of life, juvenile delinquency, and drugs. A tidal wave swept over the dikes of separation, and even the little Dutch boy got washed away. So today, the wall of separation between the church and the world is gone.

CHARACTERISTICS OF WORLDLY WISDOM

James said that there are two kinds of wisdom: a wisdom that comes from above, and one that comes up from beneath—worldly or human wisdom. It's sensual, it's psychological, it's demonic, and it is divisive. I'd like to turn again to the Amplified translation, which is quite helpful, as we've seen, in the Epistle of James:

> *But if you have bitter jealousy (envy) and contention (rivalry, selfish ambition) in your hearts, do not pride yourselves on it and thus be in defiance of and false to the Truth.* (James 3:14 AMPLIFIED)

The wisdom of the world is characterized by envy and jealousy. The word for envy here is *zelos*, and we get our word "zeal" from it. In this context, it actually means "jealousy, factions, divisions." May I be very personal and say that it means this business today of dividing up the body of Christ and taking sides around personalities or issues. A wife came home from a missionary meeting and said to her husband, "Did you know that the So-and-so's are having a lot of trouble? Everybody in the church has taken sides." The husband interrupted her and said, "I suppose there are a few really odd characters in the church who are minding their own business!"

Strife and bitterness are certainly not the fruits of faith, but the tongue can stir up that kind of thing. James made a contrast between the tongue of the foolish believer and the tongue of the wise believer. In fact, as we've already seen, an uncontrolled tongue raises the question in the minds of others whether a man is a child of God or not. You cannot make me believe that a genuine believer can curse six days a week and then sing in a choir on Sunday. He cannot tell dirty jokes and then teach Sunday school, telling about the love of Jesus. That tongue you have can do either one, but if it does both, it is that which stirs up strife.

> *You cannot make me believe that a genuine believer can curse six days a week and then sing in a choir on Sunday.*

Earthly

Let's keep on reading:

> **This [superficial] wisdom is not such as comes down from above, but is earthly, unspiritual (animal), even devilish (demoniacal).** (James 3:15 AMPLIFIED)

Strife and envying do not originate with God. The wisdom of the world is "earthly"; it's confined to the earth, it's limited to the world. There's a great deal that passes for spiritual in the church that is nothing in the world but earthly wisdom. James also called it "unspiritual" (sensual), *psuchikos* in the Greek, which means "human." Knowledge, you see, is not limited to man's puny brain. We feel today that something is not knowable unless somebody knows it. But there's a great deal that the human race does not know about this vast universe, God, life, and many other things that just do not happen to be in the depository of earthly wisdom today.

Demonic

James then called worldly wisdom "devilish." That's a terrific word, but it is actually "demonic." James dealt here with something that is quite interesting, but we need to read on to lay hold of it:

For wherever there is jealousy (envy) and contention (rivalry and selfish ambition), there will also be confusion (unrest, disharmony, rebellion) and all sorts of evil and vile practices. (James 3:16 AMPLIFIED)

Worldliness in the church has produced all the cults, denominations, factions, divisions, and cliques that abound today. Have you ever noticed how zealous the cults are in propagating themselves? Well, where does that zeal come from? Does it come from God? No, it comes from below; it's satanic, it's devilish, it's demonic.

I had the privilege of taking a series of lectures under Dr. Samuel Zwemer, a great missionary to the Muslim world. He was probably one of the brainiest missionaries that I ever listened to, and he said that we cannot explain the wickedness of the world as merely human. It's human *plus* something, and that is why non-Christian religions are successful. They are supernatural from beneath. They're demonic, if you please.

Causes Confusion

Note that James also said that it results in confusion. Scripture makes it very clear that God does not create confusion. The confusion we find in the world and in the church today is brought about by the work of the devil. My beloved, the brains of the world are engaged in the wisdom of the world, attempting to work out the problems of the world. Yet there is still trouble, because the wisdom of the world always produces confusion. But where God is, things are different, "for God is not the author of confusion but of peace" (1 Corinthians 14:33 NKJV).

> *Where God is, things are different, "for God is not the author of confusion but of peace."*

Good for Nothing

James also said that it leads to "all sorts of evil," but that gives the wrong impression. Actually, it means "good for nothing." It's the kind of work that is trivial, paltry, trite, and comes to nothing. Go back a few years and look at the things that engaged people's attention. Do you remember what the fad was back in the thirties? Do you remember what the fad was in the forties? How about in the fifties? We've forgotten it today, but it was in the headlines and occupied the attention and thinking of men in that day. But it was just good for nothing; wisdom of the world never really comes to anything at all.

A little boy was playing in the house and really causing trouble. Finally, his momma said to him, "Willie, why don't you be good?" to which he replied, "I'll be good for a nickel." So she said, "Why don't you be like your father, and be good for nothing?" Well, my beloved, that's the kind of wisdom that we're talking about—the good-for-nothing kind.

WISDOM FROM ABOVE

Now notice what the dean of God's University said next:

> *But the wisdom from above is first of all pure (undefiled); then it is peace-loving, courteous (considerate, gentle). [It is willing to] yield to reason, full of compassion and good fruits; it is wholehearted and straightforward, impartial and unfeigned (free from doubts, wavering, and insincerity).* (James 3:17 AMPLIFIED)

There are two places that wisdom comes from—from above and from beneath. Don't be ridiculous like the man who said to me, "Which direction is heaven?" If you want to draw a line at a ninety-degree angle from the earth and say that's the direction where God is, then you're wrong! Because if you tried that experiment on the other side of the earth, you'd be pointing in the opposite direction. A philosopher once asked a very humble Christian, "Where is God?" The Christian replied, "Pardon me, sir, but let me ask you a question first. Where is He not?" My beloved, that question has to be answered before you can answer the question "Where is God?" Don't point in a direction and say God is there. This is not a directional question.

So why does James speak of the wisdom that's from above? Because it speaks of the condescension of God! He who is so high has stooped so low in order that He might give us wisdom. What kind of wisdom? Heavenly wisdom. "If any of you lacks wisdom, let him ask of God . . . and it will be given to him" (James 1:5 NKJV). If any man lacks it, he's to ask of God, and our heavenly Father says He will stoop to give it.

A king was sitting with his counselors, busily planning strategy for a war. As they talked, he heard his own child take a tumble down the steps and give out a cry. The king immediately pushed his chair away from the counselors' table and rushed to his little boy, that he might pick him up. And, my friend, when he did that, he wasn't any less kingly. He was just as much a king as he was when he was planning the strategy of the war. And our great heavenly Father, the King of this universe, has come down in order that He might bring salvation and redemption and help His children down here, especially when they stumble and fall. God just keeps on coming down to be what His children need.

> *God just keeps on coming down to be what His children need.*

CHARACTERISTICS OF HEAVENLY WISDOM

The things that James mentioned as characteristics of heavenly wisdom are a divine enduement; you couldn't muster them up down here on earth to save your life. They are not a human acquisition at all, but they are of God.

Pure

"But the wisdom from above is first of all pure" (James 3:17 AMPLIFIED). Fundamentalists today may think they can toy with the impure because their doctrine is right, but I don't believe it. The first beatitude our Lord gave was, "Blessed are the pure in heart, for they shall see God" (Matthew 5:8 NKJV).

No honest man can say that his heart is pure. How can the heart of man, which is desperately wicked, be made clean? Paul wrote to a young preacher:

> **Not by works of righteousness which we have done, but according to His mercy He saved us, through the washing of regeneration and renewing of the Holy Spirit.**
> (Titus 3:5 NKJV)

He wasn't talking about a baptism, but about the water of the Word of God cleansing your heart! And, my beloved, if He doesn't cleanse your heart, you haven't been born again.

Let's face up to Scripture! You have to be cleansed.

Going through this world, we get dirty. But the child of God will immediately confess—"If we confess our sins, He is faithful and just to forgive us our sins and to cleanse us from all unrighteousness" (1 John 1:9 NKJV). We need more emphasis upon this business of having the Spirit of God cleanse our hearts and lives as we read the Word of God. The Bible is the best bar of soap that there is! My, all of these cleansing agents that are advertised on television! Have you ever noticed that advertisements come in two categories? One category tells us how to get dirty: drink beer and smoke cigarettes. Then the other category tells us how to get clean afterward: the soaps and the cleansers and the sprays and all that sort of thing. May I say to you, that seems to be important as far as the world is concerned. But a child of God needs to recognize that he must be pure! The Word of God is God's method of cleansing, my beloved.

Peace-Loving

This wisdom from above not only brings purity, but it is peaceable. The word as used in James 3:17 means "tranquility, peace of mind." Every Jew knew about that—their word of greeting was "*Shalom* [peace]." They've known so little of it down through the centuries, but that was what they said when they met one another. The Lord Jesus brought peace through sins forgiven by the blood of His cross. But He also said:

Peace I leave with you, My peace I give to you; not as the world gives do I give to you. (John 14:27 NKJV)

My friend, this is a peace that many Christians need today.

I once visited a bank that displayed a very unusual collection of pictures and personal letters of the presidents of the United States. I went to read what the presidents said, and it was quite interesting. I got to the one by Woodrow Wilson, and somebody had written to him about the League of Nations. In his reply, President Wilson said something to this effect: "Society cannot be made good as such. Only individuals can be made right, and then you can have a right society." I wish that all of our presidents could recognize that. You've got to have individuals born anew, my beloved, before you can have a new society. The United Nations and other international organizations try to bring peace, and they think they can do it with money. But that's not the way peace will come. Peace must come to the human heart, my beloved, and until it's in our hearts, it can never be around us.

JAMES' ANSWER

With that background, let's come again to our question—what is worldliness?—and attempt to answer it. As I'd promised, James gave the answer:

What leads to strife (discord and feuds) and how do conflicts (quarrels and fightings) originate among you? Do they not arise from your sensual desires that are ever warring in your bodily members? You are jealous and covet [what others have] and your desires go un-fulfilled; [so] you become murderers. [To hate is to murder as far as your hearts are concerned.] You burn with envy and anger and are not able to obtain [the gratification, the contentment, and the happiness that you seek], so you fight and war. You do not have, because you do not ask. (James 4:1–2 AMPLIFIED)

What is worldliness? James put it in a nutshell. It occurs when the spirit of the world (strife and conflicts and envy) gets into the church, my beloved. That's worldliness.

When the spirit of the world gets into the church, you have a worldly church. My friend, do you think it is bad out on the battlefield? Do you think it is bad out in the world? Well, it is, but inside some churches, and inside the hearts of some individuals, it is just as bad.

In the business world, there is dog-eat-dog competition. Political parties split, and one group becomes pitted against another. As capital and labor meet around the conference table, a battle is going on. In the social world, there are climbers on the social ladder who are stepping on the hands of others as they go up. In your neighborhood and mine, one family does not speak to another. Within families there are quarrels, brother against brother. Then that spirit of strife gets into the church, and *that*, my friend, is worldliness. It represents the old nature and is not Christian at all.

A man must be regenerated by faith in Christ and be indwelt by the Holy Spirit. But we (and the church) are willing to compromise with the world in order to attain our goals, and because of that, James called us adulterers:

> **Adulterers and adulteresses! Do you not know that friendship with the world is enmity with God? Whoever therefore wants to be a friend of the world makes him-self an enemy of God.** (James 4:4 NKJV)

The way of the world is to take by force what you want. There are a great many people in the church who—as they juggle for position, wanting something or striving for some position—use the same methods that the world employs. And, my friend, *that* is worldliness, according to James.

KEEPING WORLDLINESS OUT

How can we keep worldliness out of the church? Is it even possible? James said that it is.

Prayer

Let's go back and notice something James said earlier:

> **You do not have, because you do not ask.** (James 4:2 AMPLIFIED)

There must be more prayer to keep the world out of the church. As we'll see in the next chapter, James was a man who knew about real prayer. When he said we need more prayer, he knew exactly what he was talking about. Instead of having hard knees (from being down on them in prayer), we have hard heads and hard hearts. We need to pray that God will give us more hard knees and fewer hard heads and hearts. We need more prayer today to keep worldliness out.

Grace

James mentioned something else that we need: more grace.

> **But He gives more grace. Therefore He says: "God resists the proud, but gives grace to the humble."** (James 4:6 NKJV)

We cannot attain this by self-effort. Striving to overcome is still striving, if you please. We need the kind of faith that Joshua had when he marched around Jericho.

Through Joshua's faith, the walls of Jericho fell down when they were compassed about seven days (see Joshua 6). "And this is the victory that has overcome the world—our faith" (1 John 5:4 NKJV).

We need more grace today—not the spirit of competition in the church, but the spirit of grace in our hearts to look in faith to Him. That's the way Joshua did it. He did the most absurd thing any man could do—walk around that city; but that man knew what it was to walk by faith. That's the only way to overcome the world.

Consecration

Finally, we need more consecration. James said:

> **Therefore submit to God. Resist the devil and he will flee from you. Draw near to God and He will draw near to you. Cleanse your hands, you sinners; and purify your hearts, you double-minded.** (James 4:7–8 NKJV)

Come to God with empty hands. Our problem is that we bring our plans to God and say, "Lord, here's the blueprint I've already worked out. I don't want You to change it—I'd just like to have Your blessing." And, as a result, we have worldliness in the church.

My beloved, worldliness is manifested in divisions, cliques, groups, and individuals. It's not the parties you go to, but it's the party spirit you manifest. It's not the funny hat you wear, but the hothead that's under it. It's not the painted face, but the war paint that you have on. And it's not, my beloved, the makeup that's put on the lips, but it's that gossipy tongue behind them. It's not the latest fashion that makes you worldly, but it's the last fight you started. It's not what you go to see, it's the method that you use in getting what you want. May I say to you, that is worldliness.

TEN

JAMES WILL LEAD

US IN PRAYER

J AMES WAS A GREAT MAN OF PRAYER. In fact, tradition says that he was known as "Old Camel Knees" in the early church because he spent so much time kneeling in prayer. So he is a good person to turn to for practical lessons on the subject.

James discussed three areas of prayer, where you and I live and move and have our being: prayer and wisdom, prayer and worldliness, and prayer and wellness.

PRAYER AND WISDOM

When James spoke of wisdom, he meant it in relation to the trials and troubles of this life. He was not talking about book learning or anything philosophical. Remember, James was practical, and everything he talked about in this epistle was likewise very practical. He was talking here about having wisdom regarding God's will for our lives. Notice again what he said:

My brethren, count it all joy when you fall into various trials, knowing that the testing of your faith produces patience. But let patience have its perfect work, that you may be perfect and complete, lacking nothing. (James 1:2–4 NKJV)

When James talked about being perfect, he was saying that you and I as Christians should be complete and fully mature.

When James talked about being perfect, he was saying that you and I as Christians should be complete and fully mature. In order to do that, we need to know God's will and stay in it. But following God's will requires making certain decisions. James wasn't referring to just one great decision for life, but to the many daily ones that you and I have to make—choices concerning very practical things. Shall we go here? Or shall we do that? Shall we refrain from doing this? Now, these are the things James was saying should be the matter of prayer in order to determine God's will. That's the only way we'll ever become well-rounded, mature Christians.

If we need wisdom in order to make decisions about the things that come up each day, just what are we to do when we are unsure of God's will concerning our lives? James gave us a very practical answer: we're to ask God.

If any of you lacks wisdom, let him ask of God, who gives to all liberally and without reproach, and it will be given to him. (James 1:5 NKJV)

You see, it's the everyday decisions in life that take us out of the will of God. Many of us probably start out in the morning in the will of God, but before we come to high noon, we've moved out of His will. The reason is because we were confronted with decisions to be made, and we thought we didn't need to take them to God in prayer. But, may I say to you, to know God's will we should be constantly in touch with Him, asking Him for His will concerning these matters.

Decisions face us constantly, and they are disturbing to many folks. I recall a story about a boy who got a job in a country store. The proprietor sent him down to the basement to sort potatoes. He said to the boy, "I want you to put all the big potatoes on this side of the basement and all the small potatoes on the other side of the basement. Be very careful with this—the big potatoes over here and the small potatoes over there." The boy said, "Yes, sir," and he got to work.

After about two hours had passed, he went upstairs and said to his boss, "I'm quitting." The proprietor said to him, "Son, you haven't worked but just a little while. Is the work too hard for you?" The boy answered, "No, sir. The work's not too hard." The proprietor tried again: "Am I not paying you enough?" And the boy said, "Yes, you're paying me enough, sir." So then the proprietor asked, "Well, what is it that's wrong?" The boy said, "It's all them decisions I have to make." May I say to you, my beloved, that's the problem with life today: it's them decisions that we have to make. We've all come to places where we couldn't tell the big potatoes from the small potatoes.

> *May I say to you, my beloved, that's the problem with life today: it's them decisions that we have to make.*

There are many times in our lives when we face a decision, and we don't have the wisdom to know which way we should turn. Imagine a Christian who sincerely wants to do God's will. But what *is* God's will for his life? He moves out into today and tomorrow and next week, saying, "I want to do God's will." But he comes to the crossroads of life and two ways open up to him, one to the right hand and one to the left hand. Which way shall he go? God has not put up a marker at the crossroads. He hasn't put up a signal light there that turns green for *Go* and red for *Stop*. He hasn't sent an audible voice out of heaven that says to us, "This is the way, walk ye in it." Which way are we to go, my beloved, when we come to places like that in our lives? We do not know which way to turn, and the others are blowing their horns and saying to us, "Move on!" And, friends, in life we've got to move on. But what decision shall we make?

James said, "If any man lacks wisdom, let him ask God." God is not stingy in this department—He is generous! If we look to Him for wisdom in these matters, He gives to everyone liberally. I can only speak for myself, but the highway I've come on hasn't been marked very well. I've come to many crossroads without knowing which way to turn. But I believe, my beloved, that God moves us to these crossroads purposely. If He gave us a clear road map, we'd forever be looking at that map and not be looking to Him. So He doesn't always make it clear. That keeps us close to Him, you see. But if you and I will look to Him for wisdom, He'll let us move out.

My beloved, you and I need wisdom. And if we are willing to commit matters in our lives to Him, God will lead and guide us. That doesn't mean that all in life will go smoothly. Many have difficulty. And somebody is sure to say, "But I might make a mistake and choose the wrong path." Maybe you will. Paul almost made a mistake, but the Holy Spirit prevented him from making it. Look at what happened on Paul's second missionary journey:

> **Now when they had gone through Phrygia and the region of Galatia, they were forbidden by the Holy Spirit to preach the word in Asia.** (Acts 16:6 NKJV)

At that time, Ephesus was the capital of the province of Asia. Later, Paul would do his greatest missionary work in Ephesus. But at this time, when Paul wanted to go there, the Spirit of God stopped him and blocked the way. Well, if Paul's way to Ephesus was blocked, he should have known then which way God wanted him to go, right? But he didn't.

> **After they had come to Mysia, they tried to go into Bithynia, but the Spirit did not permit them.** (Acts 16:7 NKJV)

Paul thought, *Well, if the Spirit of God doesn't intend for me to go south, He certainly intends for me to go north into Bithynia.* But the Spirit of God blocked him again and said, "Not this way."

You see, God doesn't flash green lights for us. So we need wisdom to make these decisions that confront us in life. God didn't put steering wheels on any of us for a reason—*He* wants to steer us! So when we come to the crossroads, we have a right to look to Him and ask for wisdom if we mean to do His will. And if we do take the wrong fork, that will be made clear. This is very practical. This is putting your prayers into shoe leather.

> *God didn't put steering wheels on any of us for a reason— He wants to steer us!*

PRAYER AND WORLDLINESS

We have already seen that worldliness is strife and envy. Let's review it again:

> **Where do wars and fights come from among you? Do they not come from your desires for pleasure that war in your members? You lust and do not have. You murder and covet and cannot obtain. You fight and war. Yet you do not have because you do not ask** [pray]. (James 4:1–2 NKJV)

The worldly have a desire to get, and they are willing to hurt and harm to get it. We go so far today as to build missiles and nuclear weapons in order to get what we want. That's the spirit of the world.

As James said, the worst thing that can happen is when that spirit of strife and competition gets into the heart of a believer. That is what makes a worldly Christian. God has made the heart so that only He can fill it. Even when we attempt to put the whole world in it, the heart's not filled and still longs for more. That spirit of wanting more, that spirit of getting, is what leads to carnality. That's the thing Paul spoke about when he wrote to the Corinthians:

> *And I, brethren, could not speak to you as to spiritual people but as to carnal, as to babes in Christ. I fed you with milk and not with solid food; for until now you were not able to receive it, and even now you are still not able; for you are still carnal. For where there are envy, strife, and divisions among you, are you not carnal and behaving like mere men?* (1 Corinthians 3:1–3 NKJV)

When that spirit of strife comes into the heart, it makes a carnal Christian.

But notice what James said:

> *You ask and do not receive, because you ask* [pray] *amiss, that you may spend it on your pleasures.* (James 4:3 NKJV)

The reason that our prayers are not answered is because our prayers are selfish. They are not for God's glory, but they are for our own desires, our own lusts, our own pleasures. For that reason, we must examine our prayers to see if they are genuine and to understand why we maybe didn't get the answers that we asked for. Do we pray because we have a bad case of "gimmes"? Or is it because we really want God's glory done?

He prayed for strength that he might achieve;
He was made weak that he might obey.
He prayed for health that he might do greater things;
He was given infirmity that he might do better things.
He prayed for riches that he might be happy;
He was given poverty that he might be wise.
He prayed for power that he might have the praise of
  men;
He was given infirmity that he might feel the need of
  God.
He prayed for all things that he might enjoy life;
He was given life that he might enjoy all things.
He had received nothing that he asked for—all that he
  hoped for;
His prayer was answered—he was most blessed.[1]

James said that prayer works, and if our prayers are not working, it's because we're praying as worldly Christians.

Why do we want it? Why are we asking for it? Is it because we have in our hearts the spirit of the world? My beloved, worldliness will short-circuit the power line of prayer quicker than anything else.

PRAYER AND WELLNESS

The problem of keeping well physically is one of the greatest problems we have. In fact, that's the way we greet each other, is it not? We meet somebody and ask, "How are you?" I remember as a boy in southern Oklahoma, I used to know a dear little old lady. You'd ask her, "How do you feel this morning, Miss So-and-so?" And it was either one of two things: she'd say, "I feel pert," or "I feel puny." She seemed to feel puny more often than she felt pert. A great many of us are that way. We want to enjoy good health, and we feel we ought to have it. We reason it like this: *I can be a better Christian, I can do more for God, if I am well. Therefore it must be God's will for me to stay well.* If you say that it is God's will for every Christian who gets sick to be healed, you must agree that the logical conclusion of that line of thinking is that the Christian will never die. He will be healed of every disease that causes death. May I say, that is ridiculous. Saying that it is God's will for all to be well and all to be healed is a cruel hoax perpetrated upon simple believers.

James understood that it must be the will of God in

order for someone to be healed, and I agree with him. But, again, James was very practical, and he had for us practical suggestions on what we should do when we are not well.

Is anyone among you suffering? Let him pray. Is anyone cheerful? Let him sing psalms. Is anyone among you sick? Let him call for the elders of the church, and let them pray over him, anointing him with oil in the name of the Lord. And the prayer of faith will save the sick, and the Lord will raise him up. And if he has committed sins, he will be forgiven. (James 5:13–15 NKJV)

James was not actually asking a question here. He was saying, "Someone is sick among you. What are you to do?" One thing he suggested was "anointing him with oil in the name of the Lord." There are several words that are translated "anoint" in the New Testament. One of them is used in a religious sense; that word is *chrio* in the Greek. It means to anoint with some scented unguent or oil. It is a sacred word, and it is used to refer to the anointing of Christ by God the Father with the Holy Spirit. Another word translated "anoint" is *aleipho*. It has nothing to do with ceremony or religion at all. It is used a number of times in the New Testament. In Matthew 6:17 we read, "But you, when you fast, anoint your head and wash your face" (NKJV). That use of "anoint" is cosmetic—it means simply to put something on to improve your looks. "Anoint" is used again in the Old Testament to describe putting medicine on a boil Hezekiah had on his body. So it is also used as a medical term. There's no religious value in that use of the word at all.

Now which word for "anoint" is used in James? Well, it's the medical word. It has nothing in the world to do with religious ceremony at all. It is a mistaken idea to say that this refers to some religious ceremony of putting a little oil from a bottle on someone's head, as if that would have some healing merit in it. As it is used here in James, the act of anointing has no mystical merit whatsoever. James was too practical for that. What he referred to in James 5:14 is medication. When you are sick, you are to take the medications and seek out the doctors that are available to help make you well.

But remember, James was also a man of prayer. He said, "Call for the elders [to pray]." I believe we ought to have more prayer for the sick, and I think it is God's will that we pray for them. James made this very clear:

And the prayer of faith will save the sick, and the Lord will raise him up. And if he has committed sins, he will be forgiven. (James 5:15 NKJV)

I believe you are to call on God's people to pray for you when you are sick. That does not mean God will automatically heal you. But if it is in His will, you will be made well.

I wish I could say to you that I know by daily experience, moment by moment, what it is to be completely submerged in the will of God. I'm sorry to report that many times I've held back and not been fully in God's will. But I am prepared to say this: I've been in that paradise several times. I've looked over the fence into that wonderful, marvelous garden where He wants us to walk today in shoe leather. Where you can commit your way and your will to Him completely! Where you can go out and face the world, saying, "I belong to Him. I may not know what to do tomorrow morning, but I'm committing it to Him. And if you see me stumble and fall, I want you to know I'm going to get up and brush myself off and try the other way. Because I'm committed to Him. And if I get sick, I'm going to Him in prayer, asking Him to make me well. Then I'm going to call the doctor. And if I don't get well, I'll know I have His will. And it will be the best thing in the world for me."

> *Many times I've held back and not been fully in God's will. But I am prepared to say this: I've been in that paradise several times.*

Do you need wisdom about God's will in order to make the decisions of life? Go to God in prayer. He hears, and He gives liberally. Do you have a spirit of strife within your heart today? Maybe that's what short-circuited your prayer. Do you want to be well? Every normal person wants to be well. Can we make that a matter of prayer? We certainly can. And James said that you can expect an answer from God if you do pray about it.

ELEVEN

THE CHRISTIAN
AND THE DEVIL

THE FOURTH CHAPTER OF THE
Epistle of James gives ten imperatives, or
commandments, for Christians today:

One: "Therefore submit to God" (v. 7 NKJV).

Two: "Resist the devil and he will flee from you" (v. 7 NKJV).

Three: "Draw near to God and He will draw near to you" (v. 8) NKJV.

Four: "Cleanse your hands, you sinners" (v. 8 NKJV).

Five: "And purify your hearts, you double-minded" (v. 8 NKJV).

Six: "Lament" (v. 9 NKJV).

Seven: "And mourn" (v. 9 NKJV).

Eight: "And weep! Let your laughter be turned to mourning and your joy to gloom" (v. 9 NKJV).

Nine: "Humble yourselves in the sight of the Lord, and He will lift you up" (v. 10 NKJV).

Ten: "Do not speak evil of one another, brethren" (v. 11
NKJV).

Moses came down from the mountain and gave Israel
the Ten Commandments in stone; James got up from his
knees and gave the church ten commandments in living
color.

Moses' commandments contain the ethic for the
national life of Israel; James' commandments are the tech-
nique for the individual living in the church today.

Moses' are the Ten Commandments of the Law; James'
are the ten commandments of faith.

Moses' commandments are for a corporate nation;
James' commandments are for personal living.

Moses' commandments were given against the background of thunder and earthquake; James' commandments
were given against the background of the gentle grace of God.

Moses gave the ethic without the dynamic; James gave
the dynamic with an ethic.

Moses' commandments are *do or die*; James' commandments are *live and do*.

We have been carrying through this picture of James as
the dean in God's University of life. Here James put down
disciplines for the university student, the believer. They
may be disciplines, but James was talking also about freedom. Freedom can be enjoyed only when all have it, and

freedom is not license to do or say whatever we please. Filthy language, for example, is not freedom of speech when it offends the sensibilities of others. Therefore, there must be certain disciplines.

All ten of these commandments are important, and it's difficult to consider one without considering all of them. But the one in particular that I'd like to focus on now is the second: "Resist the devil and he will flee from you" (James 4:7 NKJV). For the Christian today, this is very pertinent and practical. But we must move back and pick up the chain of thought that James was developing as he gave us these ten commandments. If we are to understand this particular commandment, it cannot be lifted out and considered by itself.

ABUNDANT GRACE

Now notice that he said:

> But He gives more grace. Therefore He says: "God resists the proud, but gives grace to the humble." (James 4:6 NKJV)

Before he ever put down a commandment for a believer, James called our attention to the abundance and availability of the grace of God to aid Christians in this world filled with temptation and sin. I have said this again and again: God is overloaded with grace. You and I just don't know how gracious He is. He has an abundance of grace.

Grace has been defined as "unmerited favor," but I call it "love in action." God didn't save us by love. He gave His Son, and it is by His grace that we are saved. You may say, "Oh, I am so wrong on the inside, so sinful." Go to Him, and tell Him you are wrong on the inside, and ask Him for grace to overcome it. He will give you the grace you need, for He has so much of it, and He is the living Christ, interceding at God's right hand for you.

> *That's the way God supplies His grace: as it's needed, and there is always more to follow.*

The story is told of a rich Christian who was very much interested in the welfare of a poor young man who was struggling financially. So the rich man sent to him an anonymous cash gift with a note that read: "This is yours, use it wisely, more to follow." In two weeks, the young man received another envelope containing money and the simple note: "More to follow." Every two weeks he received another envelope just like it. That's the way God supplies

His grace: as it's needed, and there is always more to follow. "But He gives more grace." God is able to supply the grace that is needed.

Another story that I like a lot is that of the woman from the slums of London who was having her first holiday down at the seashore. She'd lived in London all her life and had never before looked upon the ocean. When she saw the vast sea, she began to weep. Someone asked her why she was crying, and she said, "All my life, I have never had enough of anything. This is the first time I've ever seen anything that there was enough of it." May I say to you, the grace of God is like a vast ocean, and there is enough of it.

Now, some may doubt the surplus of His grace. May I say to you, all the medicine in the world cannot cure the sick; *the remedy must be taken*. Likewise, God has the grace, my friend—lay hold of it! It is possible for a man to die of thirst with a pure spring of water right before him. He has to *drink* of it, he has to appropriate it, before it can save his life. You don't blame soap and water for the fact that there are dirty people in the world, do you? There is plenty of soap and water to clean you up, my friend. A great many folks blame God when He has *more* grace. The difficulty is that they have not appropriated the grace of God in their own lives.

ONLY FOR THE HUMBLE

However, James did put down a condition: "God resists the proud, but gives grace to the *humble*" (James 4:6 NKJV). The grace of God must be carried in a certain kind of container; it must have on it the label of humility and meekness. God will never let a proud person enjoy His grace. He has more grace than you need, but if you are to get what you need, it must be placed in a humble receptacle. I remember one time trying to buy gasoline in an open container. The filling station clerk wouldn't sell it to me, because I had the wrong kind. Likewise, God will not put His grace into just any kind of container—it must be a humble individual.

A proud person cannot receive the grace of God, for He condemns pride. God has come down against pride in His Word, and yet we don't seem to be bothered about it when we see it in the church. Solomon said, "Everyone proud in heart is an abomination to the LORD" (Proverbs 16:5 NKJV). An abomination is a pretty terrible thing! In fact, pride was the sin of Satan, who dared to say, "I will exalt my throne above the stars of God . . . I will be like the Most High" (Isaiah 14:13–14 NKJV). That was also the sin of Adam and Eve, who fell to the temptation: "You will be like God, knowing good and evil" (Genesis 3:5 NKJV). Pride always opposes God.

Pride is also probably the most insane thought that ever enters into the human mind, because all we have to measure ourselves by is our own little standards. We're like the little boy who came into the house and said to his momma rather excitedly, "I'm as tall as Goliath. I'm nine feet tall!" She smiled at him and said, "Son, how is that?" Well, he'd made his own little ruler and measured himself by it, and according to *his* ruler, he was as tall as Goliath. There are a lot of people like that today. But the grace of God can be poured only into a humble vessel, if you please. So we need to humble ourselves.

The word used in James 4:6 for "humble" is very startling. In the Greek, it means "degradation." In fact, it's one of the lowest words imaginable; it is used to describe a person at the very bottom rung of any social or moral ladder. It was the Christian writers who took that word, lifted it up, and made it something noble. Pagans don't see humility as a virtue. We have many vain and proud individuals in high places and in all walks of life. It is natural for the human animal to be lifted

> *It is natural for the human animal to be lifted up by pride, but God will bring us down.*

up by pride, but God will bring us down. He said concerning Edom:

> **"Though you ascend as high as the eagle, and though
> you set your nest among the stars, from there I will
> bring you down," says the LORD.** (Obadiah 4 NKJV)

God's grace may be as a vast ocean, but how are we to
tap into it? We want more than just a trickle; we want the
overflowing abundance of the grace of God! Well, let me
ask you: how do you get water from a reservoir? It has to
come down by gravity. High up in the mountains are dams
and lakes. The water is brought down by gravity, and every
one of the reservoirs has to be lower than the lakes, or you'd
never get the water. Does that tell you anything about the
great reservoir of the grace of God? How are you going to get
it? Well, you've got to humble yourself and get down low,
my friend. You have to get down where it can come to you,
if you please.

SUBMIT TO GOD

That is the background we have for the first commandment
given by James: "Therefore submit to God" (James 4:7
NKJV). That command follows God's requirement to receive
His grace. As I've said before, James was a practical man; he

really put the teeth of reality into what he said—he gave us something we can bite into. Why today do we have a propagation of doctrine without the application to life's situations? We know more than we are practicing, and what James attempted to do was take the Christian life out of the realm of theory and translate it into life.

If I've learned only one thing in my years of ministry, it's that God uses only the weak and the foolish. The Word says that He has chosen the weak and foolish things of the world (see 1 Corinthians 1:27), and I'm here to testify that is true. I have watched proud men sprout up, and then I've seen God set them aside. That's been true of preachers, teachers, singers, musicians, and even missionaries. My beloved, His grace is only for those who submit to Him. In the Greek, it is plural, "Submit yourselves," so no one is exempt. If God is to use any of us, we must submit to Him.

"Submit" here means actually "to place oneself under." May I say to you, friend, you can never fill a glass by holding it *above* the spigot. It's got to get down under. Isn't that profound? In our lives, many of us cry, "I don't experience the grace of God!" Where are you holding your little cup? Have you submitted to Him and gotten down low enough that you are under the spigot where the water, the grace of God, can run in?

James wasn't the only one to address this truth; it runs all the way through the Word of God. Simon Peter wrote,

"Therefore humble yourselves under the mighty hand of God, that He may exalt you in due time" (1 Peter 5:6 NKJV). It's a definite act, and it's to be done once and for all.

A Christian in the Congo years ago prayed, "Lord, You be the needle, I'll be the thread, and I'll follow wherever You go." The thread is not very helpful unless there is a needle ahead of it. Many Christians are not being very helpful because they are not following the Needle, if you please. We must submit to the will of God—that's the first commandment.

Now, I realize I've put a lot of emphasis on preliminaries, but they are necessary. A Christian who attempts to resist the devil on his own without first humbling himself and submitting to God is already defeated before he starts. But here we are now at our main subject, James' second commandment: "Resist the devil" (James 4:7 NKJV).

THE DEVIL IS REAL

In this "enlightened" age in which we live, many no longer believe in the devil. I once had a letter from a listener to my radio program who accused me of reverting back to the Middle Ages and saying things that are nothing in the world but superstition. I'm sure that listener wouldn't like our subject at hand, but may I say to you, the devil is a reality today. A man once told Charles Finney, the theologian and former president of Oberlin College, that he didn't believe the devil existed. It's said that Charles Finney replied, "Well, you resist him for a while, and then you'll believe in him." If you do not believe in the devil, it's because you haven't been doing any resisting. Resist him, and you'll soon find that he is real.

ACTIVE RESISTANCE

Now, the devil hates humility, and he'll attack any man who submits himself to God. Therefore, these first two commandments of James' belong together; I don't think you can consider one without the other.

The first, "Submit to God," could lead to a fatalistic notion of life—a total passivity where there is a lack of all activity. There are saints like that, and they are usually very pious, saying, "I'm just submitting to the will of God" but doing nothing. Submitting to God does require a passivity toward Him, but there must be activity against Satan. James said, "Resist the devil"—that's an action. A man who joins the army is subject to the officer above him. He salutes, says "Yes, sir" and "No, sir," and does what he's ordered to do. But he does that in order to fight an enemy. Likewise, the child of God submits to God—the Commanding Officer, the Captain of our salvation—that he might resist the devil, my beloved. You can't do it on your own. God doesn't want

> *God doesn't want zombies or a bunch of robots today. He wants believers who are alive and alert, who submit to Him, but who also resist the devil.*

zombies or a bunch of robots today. He wants believers who are alive and alert, who submit to Him, but who also resist the devil.

Martin Luther used to tell the story of the devil receiving reports from all of his demons that were in the world. One demon approached and said to Satan, "There was a group of Christians crossing the desert, so I let loose wild beasts upon their caravan, and every one of them was killed." But the devil said, "What nonsense! Don't you know that their souls were saved?" Another little demon stood up and said, "I saw a ship of Christians, so I whipped up a storm that destroyed the ship, and all were drowned." Again, Satan was unimpressed, yelling, "Sit down! That was foolish! Their souls were saved." But then a very clever demon approached and said, "I found a single Christian, and I worked on him until finally, I put him to sleep spiritually." And then the devil shouted and the night stars of hell sang together. Because, my beloved, that's exactly what Satan wants.

Passivity toward God is activity toward Satan. We are to submit ourselves to God, but *resist* the devil. The word "resist" is the Greek *anthistemi*, which means "to stand against." It is for defensive warfare, not offensive. There is no danger of the Christian's going into the camp of the devil, but there is danger of the devil coming into the camp of the Christian—that's Satan's strategy.

Satan has many names, and James chose an interesting one here: *diabolos*—*dia*, or "against," and *bolos*, "to throw." *Diabolos* is one who throws something against, and Satan is throwing mud, by the way! He accuses the Christian to God, and he accuses God to the Christian. Peter said he "walks about like a roaring lion, seeking whom he may devour" (1 Peter 5:8 NKJV), and we are to be prepared at all times. The problem with many believers is that we are not prepared to meet the enemy.

THE ARMOR OF GOD

Paul also spoke of this warfare:

> *Finally, my brethren, be strong in the Lord and in the power of His might* [that is, submit]. *Put on the whole armor of God, that you may be able to stand against the*

wiles [the stratagems] *of the devil. For we do not wres-tle against flesh and blood, but against principalities, against powers, against the rulers of the darkness of this age, against spiritual hosts of wickedness in the heavenly places. Therefore take up the whole armor of God, that you may be able to withstand in the evil day, and having done all, to stand.* (Ephesians 6:10–13 NKJV)

Again, the armor of God is not for offensive warfare, but for defensive warfare. And it's all for the front of you; there is nothing for a retreat. You'll get shot if you start running! Paul said that as soldiers of God, we are to stand. Scripture says that as pilgrims, we are to walk; as witnesses, we are to go; and as contenders, we are to run. But as soldiers and fighters, we are to stand, my beloved! The idea of fighting the devil, going out and attacking him, is wrong. Leave him alone, he'll attack you—especially if you've submitted to God and put on the whole armor of God.

FAITH IS THE KEY

Paul also said this about the armor:

> *Above all, taking the shield of faith with which you will be able to quench all the fiery darts of the wicked one.*
> (Ephesians 6:16 NKJV)

The shield of faith covers everything, and it is to protect us against the fiery darts of the wicked one.

If you have read John Bunyan's *Pilgrim's Progress*, you know that it tells the story of Pilgrim on his journey to the Celestial City. He wandered into the territory of Giant Despair, was captured, tied up, and put in Doubting Castle. Poor Pilgrim sat down in Doubting Castle and began to despair that all was lost and he would never get to the Celestial City. While he sat there in that doleful frame of mind, the angel of the Lord appeared to him and told him he had the key to his freedom from Doubting Castle. What was the key? Faith. Pilgrim put the key of faith in that great gate, swung it open, and was on his way again.

May I say to you, my beloved, many a Christian today is locked up in Doubting Castle, even though he has the key. The shield of faith is the only thing that can quench or stop the fiery darts of the wicked one. There are a great many things in this world today that plant doubts in the minds of

> *The shield of faith covers everything, and it is to protect us against the fiery darts of the wicked one.*

believers. Never has the Word of God been attacked as it's being attacked today. Never has the deity of Christ been questioned as it's being questioned today. Never has the resistance to God been as subtle and clever as it is at the present moment. But if you are in Doubting Castle, you have a key, my Christian friend. If you'll only use it, you can get out.

VICTORY IS CERTAIN

There's a great conflict going on right now that is bigger than any war this world has ever seen. It is the war that is going on between God and the devil, between light and darkness, between heaven and hell, between right and wrong. But the outcome is certain. As Paul said, "And the God of peace will crush Satan under your feet shortly" (Romans 16:20 NKJV). There may be temporary defeats, but as someone has said, "I would rather be defeated now, knowing I'm going to win ultimately, than to win now and know ultimately I'll be defeated." The outcome is sure, because the victory was won at the cross.

WHOSE SIDE ARE YOU ON?

Today the Lord Jesus Christ is enlisting soldiers. Have you enlisted? At this moment you are either on the devil's side or on Christ's side. There's no middle ground, and one thing is for sure: if you are not on the side of Jesus Christ, you are on the side of the devil. Our Lord made it very clear: "He who is not with Me is against Me" (Matthew 12:30 NKJV). He's asked for us to stand, and He's provided the grace. There's no draft, and He'll never force you. He's after volunteers.

We're probably all familiar with the classic recruitment poster featuring a very serious Uncle Sam pointing his finger over the caption, "Uncle Sam Wants You!" Well, the Bible tells me that Jesus Christ wants *you*. He wants to put you in His uniform, and—if you will just get down low enough for it to flow into your life—He will supply you the grace that enables you to stand against the devil. We live in a defensive world, but it's a world in which He has already won the victory. "In the world you will have tribulation; but be of good cheer, I have overcome the world" (John 16:33 NKJV). Have you enlisted? Do you wear the livery of Jesus Christ? Have you begun a pilgrim journey of faith and of standing as a soldier with that shield of faith?

> We live in a defensive world, but it's a world in which He has already won the victory.

TWELVE

WHAT IS
YOUR LIFE?

WHEREAS YOU DO NOT *know what will happen tomorrow. For what is your life? It is even a vapor that appears for a little time and then vanishes away.* (James 4:14 NKJV)

What is your life? Does it have meaning? Does it have purpose? Does it have direction? "What is your life?" is God's question, and it comes to you personally through James' epistle. We could even say that it is the final exam given at the end of each semester in God's University. It is a question that is repeated throughout the university of life; you and I shall continually face it, and each time, we ought to be able to answer it more completely.

What James actually asked is: "What is the kind, or the nature, of your life?" The answer to the question is: "It is a vapor." Well, then, what is a vapor? It is water in a gaseous state—that is your life. The best Greek text says not that *life* is a vapor, but *you* are a vapor that appears for a moment and then does not appear. The Greek word for "appear" is the same word for "vanish," but with a negative prefix. So James was really using the language of the magician: "Now you see it, now you don't." That is life, my beloved.

A vapor, or a fog, always attracts attention. If you drive up the coast on a clear day, the water is in the ocean where it ought to be. It is a thing of beauty as the sun sparkles on the surface, bringing up the different shades of blue. You see the whitecaps and the spray as it breaks upon the sandy shore. Night falls, and then some of that water climbs up a little ladder and becomes vapor—we call it fog. The next morning, fog shrouds the highways, and all the newscasters are talking about it. If it had stayed in the ocean, nobody would have said a word about it, but the moment it becomes fog, there are traffic accidents, planes are grounded, and it is the subject of conversation.

Immediately preceding the question "What is your life?" James talked about the getting of riches:

> **Come now, you who say, "Today or tomorrow we will go to such and such a city, spend a year there, buy and sell, and make a profit."** (James 4:13 NKJV)

He was talking about the man in the news, the tycoon of industry, the man who is out after the almighty dollar. He buys a lovely home, drives a big car, dresses his wife in ermine, and has all the comforts of life. What is that? James said it's a fog. It will be here for a little while, and then the oncoming sun will drive it away. That is life.

May I make a shocking statement? Human life, lived apart from and without God, is the most colossal failure in God's universe. Everything else serves a good and useful and long purpose. The sun in the sky is prodigal with its energy. As the earth passes before it, the sun just showers energy and life-giving material upon us. It has been doing this for millions of years, and they say it will be a few more million years before it runs down. Every created thing upon this earth serves a good and useful purpose. I think Thomas Gray was wrong when he wrote,

> Full many a gem of purest ray serene,
> The dark unfathomed caves of ocean bear:
> Full many a flower is born to blush unseen,
> And waste its sweetness on the desert air.[1]

> *Human life, lived apart from and without God, is the most colossal failure in God's universe.*

> Man does
> not always
> serve
> a good and
> useful
> purpose.

This simply is not true, because that flower blooming out there on the desert with no human eye to see it is seen by God, and it serves *His* purpose. This can be said of every created thing. But man—well, man does not always serve a good and useful purpose. Sometimes we hear it said that only man is vile. In Reginald Heber's "From Greenland's Icy Mountains" are these familiar lines:

> What though the spicy breezes
> Blow soft o'er Ceylon's isle;
> Though every prospect pleases,
> And only man is vile?

This is true everywhere today. Human life is out of joint, dislocated, and a colossal failure.

There are four amazing features about human life that reveal this. First, there is the brevity of life; second, the uncertainty of life; third, the mystery of life; and fourth, the inadequacy of life.

LIFE IS BRIEF

Consider first the brevity of life. The allotted time given to man is three score and ten. Let's play with this figure for a moment. Twenty years of this we need to reach maturity, or our majority. We need ten more to find a place in life— to get into the groove. It takes ten more to achieve success. Now forty years have gone by, and only thirty are left. Well, we will spend fifteen years in sleeping and eating, and some time must be spent in illness, so only fifteen remain. Of that fifteen, we will need five years to take the long steps downward toward the sunset of life. Only ten years to live, actually. What are ten years? What is a decade? What are seventy years, my beloved, when you measure them by the hoary mountains, the rocks of the ages that are all about us, or the immeasurable length of eternity? Someone has said that man's life consists of tender teens, teachable twenties, tireless thirties, fiery forties, forceful fifties, serious sixties, sacred seventies, aching eighties, shortening breath, death, the sod, God. Man's life is short; it is very brief.

Life is a vapor, a morning mist on the mountains, a bubble on a babbling brook, a spray on a wave breaking upon a rugged rock, a touch of the lips, the pressure of the hands, a sigh, the last note of a song or the dying sound of the organ, a tale that is told, the sun sinking into the west, a cloud. It has also been described as the flight of a bird that comes out of the darkness through an open window into a lighted room—there is the clink of the glass, the laughter, the light, the song—and then it flies out through the other window. That is life. Shakespeare used the voice of Macbeth to express this sentiment:

> Life's but a walking shadow, a poor player,
> That struts and frets his hour upon the stage,
> And then is heard no more. It is a tale
> Told by an idiot, full of sound and fury,
> Signifying nothing.[2]

The brevity of life makes man a failure in God's universe.

LIFE IS UNCERTAIN

The second thing that we would mention is the uncertainty of life. David said, "There is but a step between me and death" (1 Samuel 20:3 NKJV). As he moved out yonder through the forest with Saul stalking him, this man recognized how close he was to death. Isaiah moved it even closer when he said, "Sever yourselves from such a man, whose breath is in his nostrils" (Isaiah 2:22 NKJV). The breath in our nostrils is actually all that we have. We have no assurance that if we exhale, we shall be able to inhale again.

A man and his wife sat one evening in the comfort of their home, reading—he on one side of the lamp and she on the other. He reached around and asked, "Will you hand me that new book?" She said, "Yes, I think you will like it." As she passed it to him, he replied loyally, "I know I shall, since you liked it." Minutes passed, and after a time she asked, "Well, how do you like it?" There was no response. She waited a few moments, then repeated, "How do you like the book?" Still no response. She declared, "I think you are asleep!" She got up, went around, and looked at him. His eyes were open, the book had dropped down, and his hands were lifeless. He was asleep, but he had entered into that sleep out of which no man wakes in this life. I heard of another couple driving to Las Vegas one weekend to get married. They never thought that they would step over into eternity before they reached the place of their marriage. Oh, how uncertain life is down here.

My friend, you and I are living under the sentence of death. We do not know the moment it will come; we know only that "it is appointed for men to die once, but after this the judgment" (Hebrews 9:27 NKJV).

We are full of plans for tomorrow. Perhaps even now you are making plans for your next vacation. You have decided the exact time you will leave, traced your route on a road map, and made reservations at the places you will stop. How do you know you will be there? What is life? It is a vapor that appears, and then it doesn't appear. Who can count on tomorrow? You will spend tomorrow somewhere, but you *do not know* where.

In the Bible, there are eighteen metaphors used to express the transitory nature of life. It is called "a shadow that lengthens" (Psalm 102:11 NKJV), "water spilled on the ground" (2 Samuel 14:14 NKJV), "a weaver's shuttle" (Job 7:6 NKJV), and "a vapor" (James 4:14 NKJV). Therefore James said, "Don't talk of tomorrow, because you do not know about tomorrow." Life is uncertain.

LIFE IS A MYSTERY

Then there is the mystery of life to consider. I like the way James put it. He used these two words, it "appears," then it "vanishes." The mystery of life. James was not concerned about the origin of life; he was a realist, and he dealt with life as he found it. You may talk all you please about how you began, but there is nothing you can do about that. You are here, and James took it from there.

But life is a mystery. From where did we come? Are we seeds flung down from a swift passing comet? Are we protoplasmic matter that somehow came up through a reptile, a beast, or an anthropoid ape? Are we from below or above?

Are we mud or matter or mind? Are we personalities that have a certain walk, a certain talk, a laugh, and a smile? Do we have souls? Is a soul a function of the mind? What is our origin?

I saw a cartoon that was rather amusing. A man and his wife are at breakfast. He has come in wearing his bathrobe, and believe me, he is sorry looking—but she doesn't look much better. As she pours his coffee and looks at him, she says, "It's rather disappointing to think that you are the result of millions of years of evolution."

Man (apart from revelation) does not have the answer to the origin of life, nor does he know about the future. Death knocks, and the play is over. The curtain goes down, the footlights go off. All is silence and only darkness. Shakespeare, a man who knew the Bible, gave us this masterpiece as the words of Hamlet:

To be, or not to be, that is the question:
Whether 'tis nobler in the mind to suffer
The slings and arrows of outrageous fortune,
Or to take arms against a sea of troubles,
And by opposing, end them? To die, to sleep—
No more, and by a sleep to say we end
The heart-ache and the thousand natural shocks
That flesh is heir to; 'tis a consummation
Devoutly to be wish'd. To die, to sleep—

To sleep, perchance to dream—ay, there's the rub,

For in that sleep of death what dreams may come,

When we have shuffled off this mortal coil,

Must give us pause; there's the respect

That makes calamity of so long life:

For who would bear the whips and scorns of time,

Th' oppressor's wrong, the proud man's contumely,

The pangs of despis'd love, the law's delay,

The insolence of office, and the spurns

That patient merit of th' unworthy takes,

When he himself might his quietus make

With a bare bodkin? who would fardels bear,

To grunt and sweat under a weary life,

But that the dread of something after death,

The undiscover'd country, from whose bourn

No traveller returns, puzzles the will,

And makes us rather bear those ills we have,

Than fly to others that we know not of?

Thus conscience does make cowards [of us all].[3]

My friend, I say to you at this point, if you are not pre-pared to accept God's answer to life, you have no answer. Science has nothing to offer you, history has nothing to offer you, the universities of this world have nothing to offer you. Life is a mystery unless you are willing to accept God's answer.

LIFE IS INADEQUATE

I come now to the fourth and last point, the inadequacy of life. A very wealthy man, when he became old, reflected, "When I was young, I was poor; when old, I became rich. But in each condition, I found disappointment. When I had the faculties of enjoyment, I had not the means. When the means came, the faculties were gone." Life was a disappointment to him. Ask any man over the age of seventy who is without Christ today if he has found life to be satisfactory.

Let me give you the statements of some who have attained what this world calls fame. Jay Gould, the multi-millionaire (and in his day, it was something to be a multi-millionaire), said he was the most miserable man on earth. In the field of literature, the writer Charles Lamb said, "I walk up and down, thinking I am happy and knowing I am not." The poet Robert Burns wrote:

> But pleasures are like poppies spread—
> You seize the flow'r, its bloom is shed.[4]

Then he made it very personal:

> O life! thou art a galling load,
> Along a rough, a weary road,
> To wretches such as I![5]

And it was Lord Byron, who, while still a young man, wrote:

> My days are in the yellow leaf;
> The flowers and fruits of Love are gone;
> The worm—the canker, and the grief
> Are mine alone![6]

I have given you the statements of men who have been called successful, but who have lived without Christ and have found life to be inadequate.

Look at the masses in our day. Have they found life to be adequate? They have no home, they live from hand to mouth, they are whipped by the lash of necessity, there is a struggle for existence. There is no hope, no future. Many are lonely as they slip into some little apartment or an empty home. They go to the baseball games to see somebody hit a home run and then they can cheer, because in their littleness they will never hit a home run, yet they can enter into the success of another. They go to a football game and cheer when the player makes the touchdown, because, though they will never make a touchdown, they can enter into his triumph by proxy. They go to the movies where they sit and weep, because there they are the heroes or the heroines, while in their own worlds they are insignificant. They crawl up on bar stools and take one drink, then a second and a third that move them into an unreal world in which they do not live, and where they cannot stay. Harassed by frustrations, failures, and complexes, they are wound up like robots, mechanical toys. Then one day the spring breaks—and that is all. Men today are controlled by passions and appetites, driven like galley slaves at night to their dungeons, and these appetites and passions leap like wild beasts upon them. Men cry out against them, they hate them, they struggle, but it is a losing battle, and finally they yield. Like broken slaves, they become addicted to something.

Read the literature of this hour in which we are living. See if it is optimistic. See if there is anything in it but pessimism. My friend, look around you if you want to know the inadequacy of life. Hospitals are crowded, people are in pain and agony, jails are filled, mental institutions have waiting lists. Is this the best that our governments and aid societies have to offer? Then, my friend, I want none of it. I want something *better* than this.

The history of man attests to the fact that we cannot have peace. It is a story of blood and battle, tyranny and political chicanery, hatred and strife. The twentieth century brought so much, but it also took so much—the First World War, then the Second

> *The history of man attests to the fact that we cannot have peace.*

World War, and now we are ready for the Third World War. You say that it is a dark picture. I agree with you; without Christ, it *is* a dark picture. Oh, the inadequacy of our lives!

THERE IS A SOLUTION

James did not stop with the question "What is your life?" nor with the answer "It is even a vapor that appears for a little time and then vanishes away." He went on to suggest a solution:

> **Instead you ought to say, "If the Lord wills, we shall live and do this or that."** (James 4:15 NKJV)

Until you bring God into your life, until you invite Christ into your heart, your life is meaningless. I do not care in what direction you go, or what your goal might be—your life is meaningless without Jesus Christ. A life with meaning and purpose and satisfaction is a Christ-controlled life, a life surrendered to the will of God.

Jesus Christ is the answer to the *brevity of life*. He can give eternal life, because on the cross, He paid the penalty for our sin.

> **For the wages of sin is death, but the gift of God is eternal life in Christ Jesus our Lord.** (Romans 6:23 NKJV)

Do you want your sins forgiven? Do you want peace of mind?

> *"Come now, and let us reason together," says the* LORD, *"though your sins are like scarlet, they shall be as white as snow; though they are red like crimson, they shall be as wool."* (Isaiah 1:18 NKJV)

Once He has taken care of the sin problem, you will find that He has the answer for every other problem in your life.

He is also the answer for the *uncertainty of life*, for a life in the will of God is a secure life.

> *Who shall separate us from the love of Christ? Shall tribulation, or distress, or persecution, or famine, or nakedness, or peril, or sword? As it is written: "For Your sake we are killed all day long; we are accounted as sheep for the slaughter." Yet in all these things we are more than conquerors through Him who loved us. For I am persuaded that neither death nor life, nor angels nor principalities nor powers, nor things present nor things to come, nor height nor depth, nor any other created thing, shall be able to separate us from the love of God which is in Christ Jesus our Lord.* (Romans 8:35–39 NKJV)

Christ is the answer to the *mystery of life*. Man was created by God Himself, in His own image, and for His purpose.

> *Then God said, "Let Us make man in Our image,*
> *according to Our likeness; let them have dominion over*
> *the fish of the sea, over the birds of the air, and over the*
> *cattle, over all the earth and over every creeping thing*
> *that creeps on the earth." . . . And the* LORD *God*
> *formed man of the dust of the ground, and breathed*
> *into his nostrils the breath of life; and man became a*
> *living being.* (Genesis 1:26; 2:7 NKJV)

Though the image has been defaced and the dominion lost through sin, "if anyone is in Christ, he is a new creation; old things have passed away; behold, all things have become new" (2 Corinthians 5:17 NKJV).

The Lord Jesus Christ is also the answer to the *inadequacy of life,* for He can give you an abundant life. He said:

> *I have come that they may have life, and that they may*
> *have it more abundantly.* (John 10:10 NKJV)

Some of the disciples of John the Baptist came after Jesus, apparently following Him for some distance. Finally, He turned around and asked, "What do you seek?" Actually, what He said was more like this: "What are you after? What do you really want?" They replied, "Where are You staying?" intimating, "Couldn't we go home with You and talk it over?" Notice His reply, "Come and see." (See John 1:37–39.)

His invitation is the same to you today: "Come and see." After more than twenty centuries that have produced no adequate answer to life, wouldn't you like to talk it over with Him?

What do you really want? What are you after? Where are you headed? What is your life?

NOTES

Chapter 1
1. Author unknown.

Chapter 2
1. Isaac Watts, "When I Survey the Wondrous Cross."
2. Charles Wesley, "O for a Thousand Tongues."

Chapter 3
1. Author unknown.

Chapter 4
1. William Shakespeare, *Julius Caesar*, 1.2.140–141.

Chapter 5
1. Charles H. Spurgeon, *The Salt-Cellars*, 2 vols. (New York: A. C. Armstrong & Son, c. 1892).

Chapter 9

1. William Thackeray, *Vanity Fair* (London: Bradbury and Evans, 1848).

Chapter 10

1. Author unknown.

Chapter 12

1. Thomas Gray, "Elegy Written in a Country Churchyard," lines 53–56.
2. William Shakespeare, *Macbeth*, 5.5.25–28.
3. William Shakespeare, *Hamlet*, 3.1.55–82.
4. Robert Burns, "Tam o'Shanter," lines 59–60.
5. Robert Burns, "Despondency: An Ode," lines 4–6.
6. Lord Byron, "On This Day I Complete My Thirty-Sixth Year," lines 5–8.